PUTTING EDUCATION TO WORK

PUTTING EDUCATION TO WORK

How Cristo Rey High Schools
Are Transforming Urban Education

MEGAN SWEAS

HarperOne
An Imprint of HarperCollins*Publishers*

HarperOne

HarperCollins books may be purchased for educational, business, or sales promotional use. For information please e-mail the Special Markets Department at SPsales@harpercollins.com.

HarperCollins website: http://www.harpercollins.com

HarperCollins®, ®, and HarperOne™ are trademarks of HarperCollins Publishers.

FIRST EDITION

Designed by Jessica Shatan Heslin / Studio Shatan, Inc.

Library of Congress Cataloging-in-Publication Data is available upon request.

ISBN 978–0–06–228801–1

14 15 16 17 18   RRD (H)   10 9 8 7 6 5 4 3 2 1

Contents

Preface

This book is in some ways a follow-up to the first book written about Cristo Rey: *More Than a Dream* by G. R. Kearney, which told the story of how we started the first Cristo Rey school. One important idea from the start of Cristo Rey Jesuit High School in Chicago in 1996 was that the corporate work-study program was started solely to help pay the bills so that students from families who could not afford it could attend a Catholic college-prep high school.

We did not appreciate until later how working in a law firm or hospital or insurance company would transform our students and make them aspire to something greater, both in high school and in college.

That has been the greatest gift of Cristo Rey. It has captured the imagination not only of the students but of executives and employees at more than two thousand companies who want to see youth from the inner city become skilled members of the workforce. It has led forty university partners throughout the country to collaborate with Cristo Rey because our graduates help them meet their missions.

Cristo Rey has become a national movement that is inspiring school reform throughout the United States. Our job skills training program is even inspiring those who serve the poor around the world, from Fe y Alegría schools in Latin America to refugee schools in South Sudan.

More Than a Dream focused on one Cristo Rey school, the first one. This book tells the story of how that one school led to the opening of twenty-eight schools now serving more than eight thousand students. All of these schools share the same mission—to transform urban America one student at a time.

—John P. Foley, SJ
Founder of the first Cristo Rey Jesuit High School
and first president of the Cristo Rey Network

Introduction

Breakthroughs in a Broken System

A senior at Cristo Rey Jesuit College Preparatory School in Houston, Texas, Matias Esparza is lanky, with thick black hair and thin-rimmed glasses. On first impression, he seems unassuming and nerdy, speaking quietly while his classmates joke and laugh around him. But he is also a leader—the type of student who not only earns good grades, but also tutors his classmates. When he gets up on the stage to deliver his valedictorian speech at the school's inaugural graduation, he is greeted by the enthusiastic applause of his classmates and more than a thousand guests.

Although there are Cristo Rey Network schools in many cities around the country, Houston has wholeheartedly embraced the Cristo Rey model of Catholic education. The school has raised more than $20 million, and it receives 400 applications a year for just 160 spots.

The entire city seems to be at the graduation too. The Bayou Music Center is set up to seat thirteen hundred, and only the back corner is not full. Many families arrived more than an hour early and waited patiently in the Houston heat, so that they could stake out general admission seats just behind the graduates. Corporate sponsors and well-heeled supporters deferred to the families, filling in the back sections. Latecomers filed into the balcony, though the school had not planned to use it.

On a stage typically reserved for rock stars, Matias stands tall in the bright lights and greets the dignitaries on the stage. He looks comfortable in his black gown, yellow cape, and black mortarboard, casually brushing back the tassels that keep falling in his eyes.

He starts his speech with a quote. "When she was just a girl, she expected the world. But it flew away from her reach. So she ran away in her sleep and dreamed of para-para-paradise," he says, slowing the final word. Then, in a low baritone, he begins to sing—a cappella: "Para-para-paradise, every time she closed her eyes."

The crowd laughs and shouts while Matias smiles onstage. As the applause ends, Matias takes a serious tone. He can relate to the girl in his favorite song, "Paradise," by the band Coldplay, which has played on the same stage. As a boy, he thought his mom could provide all the toys he and his younger brother wanted. "Then," he says, "the concept of money and the reality that we did not have any sank into my childish brain. I knew that no matter how hard

I worked, paradise would be just out of my reach." For Matias, paradise was education.

It is an all-too-common narrative in inner-city neighborhoods. As a journalist who has both worked with youth at urban schools and written about the challenges they face, I have seen too many young people whose dreams seem out of reach. Others do not even dare to dream. At a public high school close to Cristo Rey Jesuit, fewer than 60 percent graduated in 2010, and of those only 14 percent were ready for college.[1]

A number of Matias's classmates are sure they would have ended up dropping out of high school if they had gone to a public school. Even Matias says he did not aspire to college as a high-school freshman. But the Cristo Rey model of education is changing the narrative. Thanks to his high school, Matias has found his paradise: he has a full-ride scholarship to Rice University.

The inaugural graduation in Houston celebrates the sixty individual success stories of Matias and his classmates, but the graduates also know that they are part of a bigger story. Their graduation day also represents the culmination of lessons learned over the history of the Cristo Rey Network.

AN INNOVATIVE EXPERIMENT

In Houston and across the country, Cristo Rey Network schools have helped thousands of boys and girls realize their potential. With twenty-eight schools and counting, this model of urban Catholic secondary education has come a long way since the first school opened in Chicago's Pilsen neighborhood in 1996. Back then, the school's first classes were taught in the corners of the gymnasium in a former Catholic grammar school.

Today, Cristo Rey schools still make their home in a variety of school buildings, some in better shape than others. The decrepit state of the school in Houston was a blessing in disguise—it was cheaper to rip out its institutional brick, giving its hallways a hip, loftlike feel. In Newark, students repainted their classroom walls in cheery colors, though green institutional brick still lines the hallways.

In Boston, the former Catholic grammar school feels small for teenagers, but the hardwood floors and white walls have lasted more than a hundred years and look as though they will last another hundred. In Waukegan, Illinois, meanwhile, the school building is falling apart. When the president says they are on a sinking ship, he means it literally, pointing to where the floor has sunk below a door frame. At the other end of the spectrum is Cristo Rey Jesuit High School–Twin Cities, which hardly looks like a school, with its glassed-in atrium and flexible teaching spaces. It shares its facilities, including a huge gym and state-of-the-art auditorium, with a youth center called the Colin Powell Center.

Along with their physical differences, the schools have their own unique populations—from Mexican immigrants in Chicago's Pilsen neighborhood to African-Americans on the same city's West Side. Boston has Dominican immigrants, and the Twin Cities have Somali Muslim refugees. Some schools compete for students with high-performing charter schools. As in Houston, many schools are surrounded by public schools with high dropout rates. Newer Cristo Rey schools tend to be found in states with school-choice programs.

Despite different appearances and obstacles, schools look for similar qualities in students. Although each student has his or her own unique story, Cristo Rey schools enroll students who are from low-income families, are behind in school, and are uncertain about their future. Four years later, students graduate confident and college ready. The schools boast a 100 percent college acceptance rate for seniors, and the vast majority of graduates matriculate at two- or four-year institutions within a year of high school, at rates equal to those of the highest-income Americans.

To create consistently strong outcomes across a national network of schools, the Cristo Rey Network has transformed an experiment run out of a gym into an innovative model of high-school education. It has combined the best of Catholic education with the lessons of education reform, advancing our understanding of what works best for educating disadvantaged youth.

A New Kind of Catholic School

By the time a group of Jesuit priests started thinking about a new college-prep school in Chicago in the 1990s, Catholic schools had successfully helped generations of immigrants achieve economic success. During the middle of the twentieth century, working-class parents sent their children to affordable Catholic schools,

staffed largely by women religious. The curriculum was strong
and the discipline was firm, preparing Irish, Italian, Polish, and
other European Catholics to go to college and rise into the middle
class. Catholic schools followed their pupils into the suburbs, while
African-American families and new immigrants, mostly from
Latin America, took their place in inner-city neighborhoods.

Such was the case in the Pilsen neighborhood in Chicago, just
southwest of downtown. Originally a Czech enclave, it was a pre-
dominately Mexican neighborhood by the 1980s. Pilsen's public
high schools were overcrowded, and many students dropped out
before graduation. Few who graduated were adequately prepared
for college or a career. Catholic schools, meanwhile, had lost their
free labor with the decline of religious orders and had grown too
expensive for most low-income immigrant families. St. Ignatius
College Prep, a prestigious Jesuit school, is not far from Pilsen, but
only a few of the best students from Pilsen had access to scholarships to attend the school.

As principal of St. Ignatius in the late 1980s, Father Brad
Schaeffer, SJ, thought the Jesuits should really be in Pilsen. The
Jesuits are missionary priests and, as such, belong where the need
is greatest, he thought.[2] When he became the leader of the Chicago province of Jesuits in 1991, he set into motion a plan to open
the first Cristo Rey College Preparatory School in Pilsen.

As all planning committees for Cristo Rey schools now do, the
first step toward opening the school was to conduct a feasibility
study. Schaeffer recruited a young priest, Father Jim Gartland,
SJ, to talk to hundreds of community members. After confirming
Schaeffer's intuition that Pilsen needed a high school, the Jesuits

turned to Rick Murray, a real-estate attorney and developer, to see if he could help them figure out how to fund it.

Murray took inspiration from his own progressive high-school experience, which involved service internships as a teacher's aide, a carpenter, and a bus supervisor as well as a for-credit internship at a stockbroker's office. For Murray these were unpaid, but he proposed that the students of the future Cristo Rey school work for their tuition.[3] The Jesuits hired him as a consultant to figure out how such an idea would work logistically and legally. He came up with a detailed plan for a work program in the fall of 1995. A year later, that plan was implemented when Cristo Rey Jesuit High School opened its doors, and it remains in force today. More than eight thousand students collectively earn more than $40 million each year working for two thousand companies, from family firms to Fortune 500 companies.

The corporate work-study program essentially operates as a temporary employment agency in the middle of a high school. In exchange for a set fee, companies contract with the work-study program to staff entry-level jobs. Each job is split between four student workers. After a summer training program to prepare the teenagers for a corporate environment, one-fourth of the students head to work on the first day of school, while the rest take their academic classes. Each student in a group of four works on a particular day of the week, and the fifth day is split between the group so that students work five full days in a month. Their classes are not held on their day of work, so they do not miss any schoolwork, and their school days are longer to make up for some of the lost classroom time.

At work, students perform entry-level assignments, such as filing and data entry. For the companies, hiring students is both altruistic and economical. The students are cheap, reliable labor. The work-study program handles any tax withholdings and maintains worker compensation insurance.

Although Murray's original plan called for a school budget relying almost entirely on work-study revenue, the model has evolved. Today, the goal for a Cristo Rey school at its optimum enrollment is to cover most of its operating budget with corporate work-study revenue. Fund-raising accounts for another 30 to 40 percent, and tuition covers about 10 percent. A growing number of Cristo Rey schools are in states with school-choice programs, which give them access to private-school vouchers and tax-credit programs.

From the first press conference announcing the school project, Schaeffer saw the beginnings of something big: "We hope and we believe that this will be a national model for urban Jesuit education," he said.[4] But at the time, the Jesuits still saw the innovative work program as simply a funding mechanism.

REFORMING EDUCATION

Whether or not the priests and businesspeople who founded Cristo Rey were aware of it at the time, they were entering a larger story. The story of education reform can be traced back to 1966, when social scientists concluded that family background was the most important factor determining student achievement.

The Coleman Report, named after researcher J. S. Coleman, gave many educators a fatalistic perspective. Regardless of the method of instruction, many believe that children from poor, uneducated families could not learn.[5] They held different expectations for such students, tracking them into vocational or general programs rather than academic, college-prep programs.

In the decades that followed, other researchers set out to prove this point of view wrong. To do so, they found schools that effectively taught all students, regardless of their family background. Ron Edmonds, considered the father of the Effective Schools Movement, published "Programs of School Improvement: An Overview" (*Educational Leadership*) in 1982, outlining the qualities of these effective schools.

Educators started rethinking curriculum in the 1980s based on this new understanding. Over the past thirty years, the education reform movement has advanced our understanding of how to educate students. At the heart of these reforms was the idea that all children, regardless of their background, come into school capable of learning. As the 2001 landmark educational policy said, no child should be left behind. The Common Core State Standards, being implemented in most states during the 2014–15 school year, come out of this movement as well.

As the tide shifted toward a college-prep education for all, Catholic schools proved influential. The Catholic faith told educators that all students came to them with equal capabilities to learn. Researchers looked at their college-prep curricula and focus on discipline for answers on how to effectively teach students. These qualities, plus the specific focus on disadvantaged students, positioned Cristo

Rey at the center of the education reform movement. The corporate work-study program, meanwhile, turned out to have a transformative effect on its high-school students, adding to the usual Catholic school advantages.

At work, Cristo Rey students learn persistence, attention to detail, interpersonal skills, and other qualities important to their growth. Lessons from the classroom are reinforced at work. Going into an office exposes students to new people and surroundings, and seeing what their future could hold inspires them to focus on academics and persevere through college. In recent years, researchers have made great strides in understanding how important character traits are in achieving success—in school and in life. The Cristo Rey work-study program both predates and confirms much of this research.

Business leaders might not be familiar with the academic research, but they get it. Although unemployment remains high, companies often struggle to find qualified workers. The traits and skills of Cristo Rey student workers are the qualities they look for in new employees.

Open to Growth

Like many of his classmates, Matias had the opportunity to work in Houston's energy industry at Cristo Rey Jesuit. Now, on the day of his graduation, he shares the stage with the CEO of Kinder Morgan, his corporate sponsor. Richard Kinder, a self-made billionaire, has been a major supporter of the school.

In his valedictorian speech, Matias humbly thanks Kinder and other corporate sponsors and donors, the faculty and staff, and all the family members in attendance for helping him and his classmates. "I could not have made it without all of you here," he says.

But both Matias and Kinder, the keynote speaker at the graduation, recognize one person in particular: Father T. J. Martinez, SJ, president of Cristo Rey Jesuit. Matias describes Martinez as "a little Jesuit president" who, "like the little General Napoleon Bonaparte himself, marched across Houston to talk about a new way we could offer a Jesuit college-prep education to kids like me."

Martinez may be small in stature, but he has a Texas-size personality. He's "Houston's newest source of natural energy," Kinder jokes in his speech. "At Kinder Morgan, we're trying to figure out a way to put him through our pipelines."

Many give Martinez credit for rallying Houston around the Cristo Rey model, but Martinez puts the school's historic day into a larger context. His welcome address at the graduation echoes the "Proclamation of the Birth of Christ" read in Catholic churches to begin the midnight Mass for Christmas. Rather than chanting a litany of dates, Martinez shouts into the microphone with the enthusiasm of a sports announcer building anticipation for a playoff game. "It has been 473 years since the founding of the Jesuits, and 465 years since they opened their first school," he yells.

Martinez skips ahead some four hundred years: "Seventeen years ago, the Jesuits launched a new model of high school called the Cristo Rey school."

The history is significant. Cristo Rey Jesuit in Houston and all the Cristo Rey schools across the country are successful because exceptional individuals have built upon a tradition of excellence. The Cristo Rey Network has continuously improved its model of education.

Martinez follows in the footsteps of Father John Foley, SJ, the charismatic founding president of the original school and the Cristo Rey Network. There are days for celebration, like graduation, but at a recent Network conference, Foley told his colleagues that the day we think we are good enough is the day we should close.

The following pages detail the structure of leadership in Cristo Rey schools, the logistics of the corporate work-study program, and effective teaching strategies. The stories of teachers, administrators, board members, and volunteers highlight the challenges that the schools face and capture some of the best practices employed across the Network. With twenty-eight schools open in 2014, however, these practices are neither comprehensive nor permanent. If the schools find better ways to teach math or find corporate sponsors, they will implement them—as long as the decisions are backed by evidence and data.

The book is also filled with stories of students who are studying hard, making connections at work, and realizing their dignity as children of God (in their stories, all students and families are given pseudonyms). Many students are like Matias, good students with few options. Others, as teachers like to say, do not yet know their potential. Either way, Cristo Rey students are constantly growing—personally, academically, and professionally.

Many public and charter schools successfully educate youth to be lifelong learners and leaders. The Cristo Rey Network sees its model of education not as a catchall solution, but one of the many needed remedies for the challenges of urban education. That said, all educators can learn from the Cristo Rey model of education. The appendices of the book provide helpful resources. More important than any of the specific programmatic details, though, is the key lesson of the Cristo Rey Network—its culture of high expectation. The breakthroughs in the system come from students, parents, teachers, administrators, and Network staff all continuously raising the bar. From the Network president's ambitious vision for the schools to a freshman's dream of becoming the boss in the corner office, everyone within the Cristo Rey Network aims for paradise.

PART I

How Cristo Rey Schools Work

CHAPTER ONE

The Challenge of Inner-City Education

Malik Duval has already been admitted to Cristo Rey Boston High School. Tall and lanky, he looks nervous as he walks into the school's library for a Freshman Family Visit, held in the spring of his eighth-grade year. He stands behind his taller and not-so-lanky father, Desmund, who is seeing his son's high school for the first time.

Cristo Rey Boston is in Dorchester, a diverse neighborhood just south of Boston where there are both Irish pubs and Dominican restaurants. Cristo Rey took up residence in an old parish grammar school. It is easy to imagine nuns in wimples standing in front of a blackboard and lecturing little girls in plaid skirts at the turn of the last century in the building's large classrooms. The library is a basketball court–size room with large, bright multistory windows and a stage at one end. Bookshelves line the walls and sit in one corner. Another corner serves as a computer lab, and the rest of the room is filled with tables where students work before and after school and during study periods.

Rosie Miola, an AmeriCorps volunteer working in admissions, leads Malik and Desmund to a central location a few tables away from a talkative group of students. Petite with short brown hair, Miola tries to command the students to keep it down, but Malik and Desmund hardly seem to notice the noise.

Miola hands father and son a four-page flyer about the school and asks Malik to read the mission statement. "Cristo Rey is a Catholic high school that educates young people of limited economic means to become men and women of faith, purpose, and service," he reads softly without looking up. "By offering a rigorous curriculum, a unique work-study experience, and the support of an inclusive school community, we prepare our students to succeed in college and beyond with the values essential to a fulfilling life."

Miola uses the mission statement to zero in on college. Since 2010, 100 percent of Cristo Rey Boston seniors have been accepted to four-year colleges.[1] At the same time, because the school is so focused on college, it will not be easy, Miola warns.

I like that, Desmund says. He already had read about the school online and wants a college-prep education for his son. The work-study program, he adds, will help Malik mature and see what the real world is like. But, like most people who are new to Cristo Rey, he has questions: Would Malik be able to handle a college-prep school coming from a public school? Would he have resources to help him?

Miola reassures him. "Our program is designed for students who are a little behind," she says. Malik would not be alone. Students are often two years behind according to their test scores, but the school has programs and tutoring opportunities to help them catch up.

There are more questions. How would he balance work with studies? Would he have to miss class or would it be after school? Would he be able to miss work to get help in a class?

Miola clarifies that the work program is not just a special program for students who cannot afford tuition. All students work. On the same day of the week, Malik and his classmates will go to their various work sites, and the other four days he will be in school, but with longer days than his friends in public schools. Teachers regularly stay until 6:00 p.m., and it is popular for students to stick around too. The talkative group sitting two tables away shows no signs of leaving, even though it is 4:30 on a Tuesday afternoon.

Desmund's questions reflect the challenges that Cristo Rey schools face. Urban Catholic schools have always offered low-income students a path toward success beyond high school, but today's economy brings new obstacles. Cristo Rey schools face a stubborn achievement gap; at two years behind, a typical student has to learn six years of material in four. And yet the schools' funding mechanism takes academically behind students out of the classroom five days a month. It seems like an impossible task.

Miola turns to Malik again and asks him to read the Cristo Rey vision. "Underlying the relations in our school community is the explicit belief that every student is extraordinary and capable of extraordinary things," he reads flatly, perhaps unsure of it himself.

The Achievement Gap

The vision that Malik reads out loud is rooted in the Catholic belief that all people have equal dignity as children of God. Although each Cristo Rey school is unique, a school must agree to follow ten practices in order to belong to the Cristo Rey Network. These "Mission Effectiveness Standards" were created when the Network was just forming, and school presidents continue to define and refine them. Number one, however, has remained constant: the school must be Catholic. Catholicity is at the root of all that happens within the schools, driving each of the other Mission Effectiveness Standards as well. Still, Cristo Rey Network schools have never required that students be Catholic. Like all urban Catholic schools, they have attracted a diverse set of students looking for a good faith-based education in a safe, disciplined setting. The second standard, that students must be economically disadvantaged, is rooted in a Catholic desire to serve God by serving the poor.

CRISTO REY NETWORK MISSION EFFECTIVENESS STANDARDS

As a member of the Cristo Rey Network, a school:

1. Is explicitly Catholic in mission and enjoys Church approval.
2. Serves only economically disadvantaged students. The school is open to students of various faiths and cultures.
3. Is family centered and plays an active role in the local community.
4. Shall prepare all of its students to enter and graduate from college.
5. Requires participation by all students in the work-study program. All students must be fourteen years old by September 1.
6. Integrates the learning present in its work program, classroom, and extracurricular experiences for the fullest benefit of its student workers.
7. Has an effective administrative and board structure as well as complies with all applicable state and federal laws.
8. Is financially sound and at full enrollment is primarily dependent on revenue from the work-study program to meet operating expenses. In addition, the school maintains a comprehensive advancement program to ensure financial stability.
9. Supports its graduates' efforts to obtain a college degree.
10. Is an active participant in the collaboration, support, and development of the Cristo Rey Network.

These standards explain why the students at Cristo Rey Network schools across the country share a common background. Students' families have an average household income of less than $34,000 for a family of four. At these incomes, 77 percent of the class of 2017 qualifies for a free or reduced-price lunch.[2]

Of all Network students, 96 percent come from minority communities. More than half are Hispanic, and a third are African-American.[3] The first Cristo Rey school arose out of the Jesuits' desire to serve the significant but often neglected Hispanic-American church. Nearly half of all Catholics in the United States under forty are Hispanic, and yet only 14.3 percent of Catholic-school students are Hispanic.[4]

In a city like Boston, though, Catholic schools are not the only option for low-income students. Charter schools are numerous, and Cristo Rey Boston finds itself competing for students. Cristo Rey Boston has to offer a top-notch academic program, and the 100 percent college acceptance rate appeals to applicants. Americans across the board—even parents who never finished high school themselves—recognize the importance of college today. In 2009, 73 percent of Americans surveyed said that a college degree was necessary to get ahead in life.[5]

Educational outcomes do not quite match these aspirations, but they have also improved, an indication that thirty years of education reform have been at least somewhat effective. Students at all levels are doing better, and the racial achievement gap has been closing. Still, Hispanic and black students' high-school graduation rates lag behind those of white students. In 1971, only 48 percent of Hispanic and 58 percent of black students completed high school, compared to 83 percent of white students.[6] Today, economist James Heckman, of the University of Chicago, estimates that 84 percent of white students, 72 percent of Hispanic students, and only 65 percent of black students graduate from high school.[7] (Heckman's numbers differ from many published high-school graduation rates because he takes out those who earn a General Education Degree, or GED. Those who take the GED test are disproportionally minorities, and with regard to life outcomes such as employment and income, this group's fate looks more like that of high-school dropouts than that of high-school graduates.)

Even as the racial achievement gap has been slowly closing, the achievement gap between the highest- and lowest-income students is getting worse. According to Stanford University education researcher Sean Reardon, the gap in test scores between the rich and poor is 40 percent greater today than it was thirty years ago.[8] Another study looked at graduation rates at the fifty wealthiest and the fifty poorest urban and suburban school districts. In wealthy districts, 96 percent of students graduated, while only 64 percent of students in the poorest districts earned a high-school diploma.[9]

As Cristo Rey schools know well, the problem does not start in high school. Ninety-five percent of incoming freshmen in wealthy districts were proficient in reading and math at the eighth-grade level. At high-poverty nonselective inner-city high schools, most had fifth- or sixth-grade math and reading skills, with fewer than one in five students proficient at the eighth-grade level.[10]

Catholic schools have typically offered scholarships, so that the best students from the inner city can avoid those nonselective public schools. Scholarship students mix with wealthy classmates who have had all the advantages of a private elementary and middle-school education. There are advantages to that model, and Cristo Rey schools often encourage students who have the opportunity to go to an elite Catholic prep school to do so. But scholarship spots are limited.

To make sure that Cristo Rey schools are helping the people in most need, the Mission Effectiveness Standards define "economically disadvantaged." Students' families must earn less than 75 percent of national median income. The cap can be calculated based on total income or income per person. For the class of 2017, that is $37,877 or $14,347 per family member. (Schools in particularly expensive cities like San Francisco can use their local median income.)

After addressing Malik and Desmund's concerns, Miola hands Desmund forms to fill out with the family's financial information. The second standard also requires that a third party verify families' reported finances. Desmund pulls a new smartphone out of his pocket to help him fill out the forms with the correct information, apologizing for his slowness with it. It is his first smartphone, and he is just learning how to use it, he explains. He wants to get a computer too, so that he can use it to stay in touch with the school and Malik's teachers.

Cristo Rey Boston does not require a lot of its students' parents. Still, being family centered is the Cristo Rey Network's third Mission Effectiveness Standard. All schools have online systems to help parents track their children's progress and connect with teachers.

Parents might not be involved in their children's education for a variety of reasons—some are working multiple low-paying jobs to support their children; a few are in jail. Students are often raised by single mothers or grandparents. The schools have found that students with positive outside support—a parent, grandparent, or older sibling reminding them to do their homework—are more successful in school than those without that figure. That Malik's dad comes with him to the Freshman Family Visit is a positive sign.

Miola points back to the brochure to show father and son the start date. As his father marks the first day of school in his calendar—August 12—Malik grimaces. Going to a college-prep school with a work program will require adjustments for the family and sacrifice from Malik, including some of his summer vacation.

Why College?

For past generations, computer skills and a college degree were not necessities; a high-school graduate may have been able to raise a family with a working-class job. Since the 1990s, the United States has shifted toward a "knowledge-based economy." Today, highly skilled workers who are able to create and use new technologies are the key to economic growth. The U.S. manufacturing industry, on the other hand, has lost three million jobs in the last ten years. Most of these were lost in the recession, but the industry's employment numbers had been declining since the peak in 1979, when nearly twenty million people were employed in manufacturing.[11]

Postsecondary education is becoming the standard in the knowledge-based economy. Unemployment and earnings numbers from the Bureau of Labor Statistics show the importance of education. In 2013, unemployment for those with less than a high-school degree was 11 percent, and for high-school degree holders it was 7.5 percent. For those who graduate from college, however, unemployment was only 4 percent. Moreover, income more than doubles with a college degree. The national median weekly income is $472 for a high-school dropout, $651 for a high-school graduate, and $1,108 for a college graduate.[12]

The recession has intensified the gap in unemployment based on education levels. The economy has largely recovered for those with postsecondary education, but it has not for those without, according to education researcher David Conley. He estimates that 5.6 million jobs were lost in the recession for those with a high-school diploma or less, and these jobs largely have not returned.[13]

Much of the country has kept up with—and pushed along—these economic forces. Americans are going to college in increasing numbers. Today, 33 percent of those between twenty-five and twenty-nine years of age have a four-year college degree. Although such a number might seem low, it is up from just 12 percent in 1971.

The racial and socioeconomic achievement gaps in K–12 education, though, continue through college. Although 40 percent of white Americans have college degrees, only 23 percent of African-Americans and 15 percent of Hispanic-Americans do. Fifty-four percent of children from families in the highest income quartile complete college, while only 9 percent of children from families in the lowest income quartile graduate.[14] "The influence of parental wealth is stronger in the United States than anywhere else in the developed world," a Council on Foreign Relations report on education points out.[15]

Whether Malik goes to college concerns more than just him and his family. The Council on Foreign Relations links the equality of educational opportunities to U.S. economic success and national security.[16] Some argue that not everyone needs a college degree, but even those high-school graduates who do not go to college benefit from a college-prep education; experts have found that preparing students for college also prepares them for success in the workforce.[17] Aiming high makes for a sound national policy.

From the beginning of the Cristo Rey Network, there have been debates about what student success looks like. The fourth and ninth Mission Effectiveness Standards say that a Cristo Rey school "shall prepare all of its students to enter and graduate from college" and "support its graduates' efforts to obtain a college degree." But if a graduate becomes a skilled craftsman or gets a certificate in therapeutic massage rather than going to college, is that not a success?

Regardless, the schools want their students to know that they *can* succeed in college and beyond. Aiming high is a defining characteristic of the schools.

The Evolution of Catholic Education

The school that Malik Duval plans to graduate from in 2017 is much different from the one that converted to a Cristo Rey school in 2004. Cristo Rey Boston opened as St. John's High School in 1921 with the purpose of serving Boston's Catholic immigrant communities.[18] Later it took the name North Cambridge Catholic.

Few Americans went to secondary school before the turn of the twentieth century. Parish grammar schools had been around for years, but the only Catholic secondary schools had been for boys preparing for seminary. Orders of nuns, meanwhile, ran girls' academies mostly for upper-class families. As educational opportunities expanded, the church also started opening high schools for its members. Because Catholics tended to be immigrants who settled in cities, the church built schools near them. Catholic secondary education began in service of low-income families living in the inner city.[19]

Throughout the twentieth century, secular educators debated about what public secondary education should look like, whether it should be a classical curriculum preparing students for college or a vocational program preparing students for the workplace. Educators largely accepted the idea that children's potential differed based on the capabilities and resources of their families. Public high schools, therefore, adopted a "comprehensive" approach to education in the 1960s and 1970s, offering students different tracks depending on their post-high-school plans. College-bound students took an academic track, while those planning to go straight into the job market took classes in a vocational track. A third track was developed that offered lighter academic and lifestyle classes like "Checkbook Mathematics" or "Personal Grooming and Fashion."[20] This general education track was considered relevant and sensitive to "the needs of disadvantaged students."[21] In practice, tracking resulted in discrimination. Poor and minority students often found themselves in general and vocational tracks, limiting their ability to go to college or into professional fields after high school.

Although some Catholic schools were influenced by the trend toward general and vocational tracks, they typically stuck with a consistent college-prep curriculum. *Catholic Schools and the Common Good,* by Anthony Bryk, Valerie Lee, and Peter Holland, was one of the seminal studies on the effectiveness of Catholic secondary schools. It describes the three main reasons Catholic schools continued to offer a college-prep education while public schools offered other tracks. Most significant was the belief, intrinsic to the Catholic faith, in the equal human dignity of every person. All deserve and are capable of receiving a classical education that advances their spiritual understanding "Developing the student's ability to reason was a central tenet of Catholic educational philosophy," the study's authors conclude. "Such intellectual development was deemed necessary in order to grasp fully the established understandings about person, society, and God."[22]

But there were also practical concerns. Catholic secondary schools wanted legitimacy from Catholic colleges. And though they may not have had access to secondary education themselves, parents saw the value in preparing their children to attend Catholic colleges. "An academic education in high school and then college paved the way for social position, the professions, and Catholic leadership in society," according to Bryk, Lee, and Holland.[23]

This is what St. John's and then North Cambridge Catholic did for its students. Graduates went on to become business and civic leaders locally and nationally. Its most famous alum, Thomas P. O'Neill Jr., graduated from St. John's in 1931, went on to Boston College, and was elected to the U.S. House of Representatives in 1953. "Tip" O'Neill, as the Democratic politician is better known, served as Speaker of the U.S. House of Representatives in the 1980s.[24]

During the years that O'Neill served in Washington, Boston and his alma mater were changing. The school moved to a new campus and became North Cambridge Catholic in 1957. O'Neill's son, Thomas P. O'Neill III, or Tommy, as he is known by friends, graduated from the new campus in 1962, just as the Second Vatican Council was beginning to open the church to the modern world.[25] By the time Tip O'Neill rose to Speaker, his alma mater looked very different.

Cambridge gentrified during these years. Local residents were no longer poor Catholic immigrants, and with more resources from wealthier residents public schools became stronger. North Cambridge Catholic began to search farther afield to fill its seats, recruiting Latino, African-American, Cape Verdean, Haitian, and Vietnamese students from other parts of Boston. "These students did not have the tools, the resources, the educational background, the training they needed to be successful in a high school," says Jeff Thielman, who became president of Cristo Rey Boston after helping start the Cristo Rey Network.

The socioeconomic achievement gap starts before students enter kindergarten, according to Reardon, the Stanford researcher.[26] Contrary to the idea that family predetermines academic achievement, he finds that test scores are improving across the board, including for low-income students. Still, Reardon attributes the widening achievement gap among socioeconomic groups to the inability of low-income parents to invest as much time and money in their children's cognitive development as wealthier parents do.

Even so, Catholic schools have successfully helped low-income students catch up. *Catholic Schools and the Common Good* analyzed research from the 1980s and concluded that "average achievement is somewhat higher in Catholic high schools than in public high schools, and . . . Catholic high schools may be especially helpful for disadvantaged students."[27] Even when controlling for class, the study found higher achievement in Catholic schools.

The study largely credited Catholic schools' effectiveness to their academic focus. Only 10 percent of Catholic school students were on a vocational track.[28] Further, it found that Catholic schools were not simply accepting the best, most motivated students. Students were on the academic track not because they saw themselves as capable of it, but because the school assigned them to that track.[29]

Those who were on vocational or general tracks in Catholic schools also took more academic courses than their public-school counterparts.[30] For instance, only 4 percent of Catholic schools offered wood or machine shop, while 89 percent of public schools did so. Meanwhile, 80 percent of Catholic schools offered calculus compared to 47 percent of public schools.[31] Catholic schools' decision to concentrate on academics was both philosophical and economic. They had limited resources, and they spent them on academic programs.

More Than Money

Even as researchers lauded their academic programs, Catholic schools were in danger. The question about Catholic education was not what happens in the classroom, but how to fund it.

From 1967 to 1990, religious staff at schools dropped 79 percent.[32] In 2014, the National Catholic Education Association reports that only 3.2 percent of Catholic school staff are religious.[33] Without the priests, brothers, and women religious who worked for free, the cost of Catholic schooling soared. In 1967, the average tuition for a Catholic secondary school was $203, or about $1,420 in today's terms.[34] In 2013, the average tuition for a Catholic high school was $9,612.[35] Higher tuition meant fewer students enrolled in Catholic schools. Enrollment at Catholic schools dropped from its height of more than 5.2 million students in the 1960s to less than 2 million in the 2013–14 school year.[36] The loss of students only intensified schools' financial problems.

Dioceses were able to bankroll some schools where tuition could not cover expenses, but more often than not schools were forced to close. In 2001, the Boston archdiocese announced that schools would have to be financially self-sufficient by 2004.[37] If North Cambridge Catholic could not find another way to support itself, it would have to close.

The news that there was a financially viable model of Catholic secondary education in Chicago traveled quickly across the Catholic world. A nascent Cristo Rey Network received requests to start new schools and save existing ones from all around the country. Today, only a handful of Cristo Rey schools have been converted from existing Catholic high schools, and the Network no longer accepts conversions as a policy. Embracing the Cristo Rey model is not easy for an existing school.

But in those early days of figuring out how to replicate the model, both the Network and the Boston school were confident that they had found the solution to the school's financial problems. The difficulties North Cambridge Catholic faced in becoming Cristo Rey Boston show just how different a Cristo Rey school is from a traditional Catholic high school. With the population it served, the partnership seemed like a natural fit, but something was amiss.

Carrie Wagner started as a new high-school teacher at North Cambridge Catholic in 2001 and loved it. "I wanted very much to be in urban education," she says. "We felt like we were doing a great job."

Her students were not just poor, though—they often had been kicked out of other schools. "We knew we were a school of last resort," Wagner recalls. "In retrospect, I see that our mission was very much an affective one rather than an academic one. We would take anyone, and everyone graduated."

Some North Cambridge Catholic students went on to college, but others went on to working-class jobs, which was acceptable to most teachers. The idea that not all students can learn past a certain predestined point seemed to have spread from public schools and infected North Cambridge Catholic. Staff "did not believe students could achieve at higher levels and were not taking responsibility for student learning," Jeff Thielman wrote in a case study on the school. "A good teacher was one who could maintain discipline in the classroom."[38]

Teachers had free rein over their own classrooms, resulting in a wide variance in expectations. They were rarely observed and did not receive the feedback they needed to grow. Teachers might have looked at test scores to see how individual students had done, but there was no systemic analysis of test scores that could be used to improve instruction.[39] "At the time, we made a lot of excuses— 'Our students aren't good test takers,'" Wagner confirms.

Some teachers wanted to improve the school. Wagner was part of a committee that met weekly to discuss issues that the school faced. "But with very little administrative support, there was only so much we could do," she says.

Joining the Cristo Rey Network gave the school a new level of accountability, requiring it to report results such as test scores, graduation rates, and college enrollment. In addition, teachers gained access to a pool of knowledge and professional development opportunities through the network of schools.

Thielman credits the high expectation of students in the workplace for early successes of the converted Cristo Rey school. "The work-study program all of a sudden raised the stakes," he theorizes. In 2004, just 29 percent of students enrolled in two- or four-year colleges. After just a few years of being a Cristo Rey school, 69 percent of the class of 2007 did so. Still, those numbers were not good enough for school leaders.

When Father Jose Medina became principal in 2007, he found the academic program to be lacking. Medina analyzed the test scores and found that students were graduating below grade level and not progressing a full academic year between tests.[40] For instance, in reading, as sophomores, the class of 2008 had a median score equivalent to eighth graders. As juniors, the class average rose, but was still below ninth-grade levels. By senior year, they were still below the tenth-grade level.[41]

"I had a real crisis," Wagner says. "I had been misled into thinking we were doing something valuable, and I was shocked to think we were doing our students a disservice rather than a service."

Medina implemented many components that have become standard for a Cristo Rey school—an online grading system and e-mail for teachers and students to facilitate communication, common assessments, and consistent grading.[42] The school created a curriculum designed around what would be expected of students at graduation, and each student would have to take one Advanced Placement class. To prepare students to be ready for an AP class as seniors, the freshman year program was intensified and double blocks were added for subjects like math.[43] Collaboration among teachers was promoted through weekly department meetings.[44]

The school's first class in the new program experienced impressive gains; most students advanced more than one academic level during their freshman year.[45] Today, 100 percent of Cristo Rey Boston seniors are accepted into a four-year college, and more than 90 percent enroll. The school is above the Network average for college enrollment, but it is below the Network average for ACT test improvement from freshman to senior year.[46] Still, its academic outcomes have continued, while the school has strengthened its commitment to serving the poorest of the poor, consistent with the Cristo Rey mission. The average family income dropped from nearly $42,000 for the class of 2012 to less than $24,000 for the class of 2017, the lowest in the Network.[47] North Cambridge Catholic made its full transition to Cristo Rey Boston in 2010, when it moved from gentrified Cambridge to Dorchester to be closer to the families the school serves.

Though Cristo Rey Boston had a rough start, there are lessons in its journey. Most important, it takes more than a traditional Catholic school education to help disadvantaged youth be ready for college and beyond. The safe, nurturing environment of a Catholic school and the experience of working in corporations is not enough without a comprehensive college-prep academic program and a culture of high expectations.

CHAPTER TWO

A New Vision of Administration

Cristo Rey Boston teacher Michael Kauffmann looks the part of English instructor at a college-prep high school—the sleeves rolled up on his light blue Polo dress shirt, thin-rimmed glasses, reddish hair over his ears. "A white, bearded male English teacher," he describes himself, "the least rare commodity in the entire country."

As an English, philosophy, and rhetoric major at St. Joseph's University in Philadelphia, Kauffmann was "as utterly unemployable as possible" upon graduation, so on the recommendation of a professor he became a volunteer at Cristo Rey Jesuit High School in Chicago. There he found his calling in front of a classroom of low-income urban youth. He read all he could on the philosophy of education, finding inspiration in John Dewey's idea that education could be a tool of social reform and democracy. After his two-year volunteer stint, he signed up for a master's in education program at Boston College to better learn the trade. The program was experiential, placing Kauffmann in a Boston public-school classroom. Kauffmann was ready for whatever the public school had to throw his way. "I'm going to be the one-man difference-making machine," he thought.

But Kauffmann soon found that he could not change his students' lives single-handedly. He could not even break up a fight—only certain people in the building were authorized to do so. Even the girls fought—and brutally, Kauffmann says. Though it has been a few years, his voice is still filled with surprise as he recalls three fights he had to watch while waiting for a security guard. "Girls were afraid to go to the bathroom. If you're scared to go to the bathroom, you cannot learn in that environment. You cannot concentrate on what you're doing," he says.

The violence was difficult to deal with, but the apathy was worse. "That more than anything is what got to me: students who felt they had nowhere to go in terms of a future, their heads down," Kauffmann says. "Your heart breaks at each and every one of them."

The adult community was not much better. Teachers were at war with an incompetent public-school principal, but instead of fists, their weapon was a letter-writing campaign to the superintendent. Kauffmann was sympathetic to the teachers' point of view, but disappointed by the politics. School meetings spent on political fights did not seem like a productive use of time.

"Sadly, working that one year in that public school really disabused me of the notion that one person can make a difference alone when so much is at stake. You really need an entire team, an entire building dedicated to that kind of change," he says. He knew he had to get back to a Cristo Rey school.

The effectiveness of a Cristo Rey school is rooted in collaboration and high expectations for the adult community. Strong school leadership is required to implement a rigorous college-prep education and work-study program within the context of a supportive Catholic school environment.

The administration of the school is so important that the seventh of the Mission Effectiveness Standards for a Cristo Rey school requires that each school have an effective administration and board structure, detailing the role of the board and school leaders. Parts of other standards speak to the roles of leaders in specific departments, while the eighth standard lays out the financial requirements of a school, including fund-raising and starting an endowment. Although the standards stop short of creating a flowchart for each school, they lay out the expectations for the adults running a Cristo Rey school.

The Mission Effectiveness Standards are not rules from above, though. They come out of a common understanding of the adults' work. The spirituality in a Cristo Rey school puts Jesus at the center of the Cristo Rey community at the same time that it makes room for people of other faiths to work at the schools. Building upon the message of Jesus, the schools must foster a loving community that centers on serving one's brothers and sisters.

Teachers and staff, furthermore, cannot expect from students what they do not model. "It's important to recognize that the success of a Cristo Rey school is dependent on the adult community," writes Father Robert Welsh, SJ, who helped start St. Martin de

Porres High School in Cleveland. "The adult community cannot form a student body to come to know, love, and serve Jesus Christ unless that same adult community knows, loves, and serves Jesus Christ." Likewise, if the adults want the students to work hard and support each other through challenges, the adults in the school must do so as well.

This is what was missing at the public school Kauffmann worked at for a year. Not everyone was committed to the same mission. It is an essential lesson for all schools, says Patricia Weitzel-O'Neill, executive director of the Barbara and Patrick Roche Center for Catholic Education at Boston College. Weitzel-O'Neill came to know and admire the Cristo Rey model of education when serving as superintendent of the Washington, DC, Catholic school system. "It's a model of collaborative leadership which has allowed for the schools to succeed and be sustained against all odds," she says.

From the Top

The Jesuits' first step for taking Cristo Rey from an idea to a real school in the fall of 1995 was to appoint one of their own, Father John Foley, SJ, as president of the school.[1] Foley, a charismatic priest, had spent thirty-four years in Peru working in education before his superior, Father Brad Schaeffer, SJ, asked him to return to Chicago to work on the new school project. Foley obediently agreed.[2]

At the time, only 10 percent of Catholic schools had presidents.[3]

Traditionally, the operation of a Catholic school was left to the principal, who acted like a small business owner. "No task is too big or too small for the principal to undertake, and the variety seems endless," *Catholic Schools and the Common Good* researchers found. Principals were in charge of "financial management, development and fund-raising, public and alumni relations, faculty selection and supervision, student recruitment, and in many cases, discipline and instructional leadership."[4]

But at the new Catholic school in Chicago, there was too much for the principal to do. Foley hired Sister Judy Murphy, OSB, as his principal, tasking her with the challenge of setting up a college-prep curriculum that would reach students who seemed more likely to drop out of high school than go to college. In the past, a Jesuit school would have been staffed entirely by Jesuits, but there were not enough Jesuits to go around.

In looking for the best people rather than best Jesuits to run his school, Foley wanted a layperson—someone with business experience—to figure out how the work program would function. Preston Kendall was working as an executive at an insurance company at the time, but he wanted more meaning in his career. The first time Foley invited him to tour Pilsen, Foley explained the Jesuits' plans for the school. "The problem is, how do you open a college-prep high school that's purposely for people who cannot pay for it?" Kendall remembers Foley saying to him. "We have an idea about kids working, but we need a business guy to make that happen."

In the early 1990s, changes were coming to the leadership of Catholic schools. Even as there were not enough nuns and priests to fill the classrooms, a religious order could still imbue a school with its charism by maintaining leadership. Religious orders were moving to "sponsoring" rather than "owning" Catholic schools. As governance by religious orders declined, laypeople increasingly were found not only in the classroom, but also in principals' offices and in board meetings.

Schools would be the test of the Second Vatican Council, the *Catholic Schools and the Common Good* researchers predicted. Vatican II had elevated the importance of the laity, calling the church the "People of God." Educators could put into practice the collaborative leadership that the council preached. But when the study was published in 1993, it remained to be seen how the church would respond. "Will committed laywomen and laymen continue to answer this call to service?" the researchers asked. "How does an institution appropriate the best of contemporary culture (such as principles of effective organizational management and budgeting) while at the same time maintaining its distinctive roots?"[5]

Cristo Rey seemed to answer these questions, leading the way into new forms of Catholic school governance. By fall 2004, there were ten Cristo Rey schools, marking the first year the Network opened multiple—six—new schools. Beyond the growing organization, nearly half of Catholic schools now had both a principal and a president, just like the first Cristo Rey school.[6]

Like the Cristo Rey model itself, the move toward shared leadership and lay boards was a response to the new challenges of Catholic education—dropping enrollment, lay faculty and accompanying higher salaries and benefits, and increased competition for students—says John T. James, director of the Catholic

Leadership Program at St. Louis University.[7] The Jesuits' extensive experience in higher education helped them become early adopters of administrative models used in colleges and universities. More than thirty religious congregations sponsor or endorse Cristo Rey schools today, but it was the Jesuits who were responsible for choosing the leadership model.

Studies have shown that the "president-principal model" of school leadership improves a school's fund-raising, strategic planning, and communication as well as internal issues such as instruction. By taking over a school's business operations and external relations, a president can free up the principal to focus on the quality of education. A large part of a Cristo Rey school president's time is spent not only raising funds, but also helping the corporate work-study director find job sponsors.

James suggests that the model itself works only as well as the people in those two main positions.[8] Rob Birdsell, former president of the Cristo Rey Network, saw this phenomenon when he started in August 2007. In his first few months of the job, the Network grew from twelve to nineteen schools, and Birdsell visited each one. "I was just wowed by everybody I met out in the field," he recalls.

The collaborative leadership style also requires trust. At an ordinary school, the principal and president must work well together, but Cristo Rey schools throw a corporate work-study director into the mix. If educators do not value the work program for anything more than the funding it provides for the classroom, schools will falter. Without complete buy-in from the leadership, the model will not work.

Today, the Network's policies aim to get the right people into the right roles from the start. The Network has a say in the hiring of the president, corporate work-study director, and principal at start-up schools, including the power to reject candidates. "The most critical factor in the success of a Cristo Rey school is that of leadership," reads a Network document on the "lessons learned" in its first decade.[9]

A Ministry Run by Laypeople

When researchers surveyed schools that adopted a president-principal model of leadership, only 49 percent reported they did so in order to prepare lay leadership for the school. When the Jesuits started the first Cristo Rey school, though, they were conscious of their shrinking numbers.[10] They knew that laypeople would be central to Cristo Rey's future as faculty, staff, administrators, and board members. All religious communities talk about getting laypeople more involved, but "we're doing it," Foley says. "It's a ministry run by laypeople."

Father Brad Schaeffer, the provincial of the Chicago Jesuits, first thought Cristo Rey would be a model of urban *Jesuit* education. Foley, meanwhile, envisioned the school being spread by other orders. Indeed, he challenged the De La Salle Christian Brothers, a teaching order with a mission to educate the poor, to beat the Jesuits to replicating the school at a conference. Soon, a Lasallian group planning to open a high school in Portland was calling to inquire about the Cristo Rey model.

Matt Powell, president of the planned school, visited Cristo

Rey Jesuit in Chicago in the fall of 2000. He was greeted by Jeff Thielman, then development director of the school, and a billboard reading, "Welcome, Brother Matt Powell." Thielman, who "runs a million miles an hour," Powell says, had introduced him to four people as "Brother Matt Powell" before he could correct him. Powell is, in fact, a layman.

At the time, the Jesuits would not have opened a new school and put a layperson at its head. "But the Christian Brothers wanted the mission to continue whether there are brothers or not," Powell says. In the late 1980s, they started a program through which laypeople could become partners, taking a different set of vows that exclude celibacy and poverty, but walking side by side with the brothers in their mission.

Powell and six other laypeople at De La Salle North Catholic High School have gone through significant formation in the Christian Brothers' pedagogy and spirituality. A husband and wife who are teachers at the school run a community of four Lasallian volunteers. "It's like a brothers' community without brothers," Powell says, complete with morning and evening prayer.

The trend toward lay leadership of Cristo Rey schools is similar across the Network. Of the 1,211 faculty and staff employed by Cristo Rey schools during the 2012–13 school year, only 69 were religious.[11] Preston Kendall was the only layperson in Cristo Rey Jesuit's leadership in 1996, but today all three positions at the original school are held by laypeople.[12] The Cristo Rey Network's central offices have largely been run by laypeople as well.

Along with Father Foley, Kendall and Thielman essentially started and ran the Cristo Rey Network. At first, they simply made time within their already busy jobs to help Powell and other school leaders open new schools. When the Network was formally incorporated in 2003, they moved to a separate office and passed the baton to a second generation of Cristo Rey school leaders.

Both Kendall and Thielman have since come full circle, returning to Network schools as presidents. Kendall is president at the school in Waukegan, Illinois, and Thielman took over Cristo Rey Boston High School in the midst of its academic turnaround. It is not unusual for a Cristo Rey school to be led by a lay president, and the boards of Cristo Rey schools are largely lay as well, recruited for their business skills and knowledge.

At a May 2013 Cristo Rey Boston board meeting, Thielman sat next to his board chair, Tommy O'Neill, son of former Speaker of the House Tip O'Neill and a 1962 graduate of North Cambridge Catholic. O'Neill, a major civic leader in Boston and former lieutenant governor of Massachusetts, resembles his father, with a large nose and bushy white hair and eyebrows. Thielman could not look more different, sitting to O'Neill's right in a suit and tie, with not a hair on his head. Yet the two share an enthusiasm for the Cristo Rey financial model.

O'Neill asked Father Jose Medina, the principal and the only priest in the room, to offer a prayer. It was Medina's last board meeting and two young laywomen, sitting to his left, would be taking his place as the school's academic leaders. For the benefit of these new leaders, O'Neill asked members to introduce themselves. Board members included work sponsors and businesspeople, a theology professor, North Cambridge Catholic alumni, and educators.

The board has committees for development, jobs, finance and

facilities, and academics and student life, and each provides a report at meetings. Finances were the primary order of the day. As the board considered the budget for the 2013–14 school year, money—the president's primary concern—was tight. Thielman had proposed a budget of $3.85 million, but board members worried that the school would not have the cash flow to support it, considering that some major bills would be coming due that year. At the same time, cuts would slow internal growth, Medina pointed out.

It is a constant struggle for Cristo Rey school presidents—balancing the school's need for more funds and the board's push for fiscal responsibility. As a governing board, the trustees have the final say on the budget, but with representatives of religious communities and educators on the board along with businesspeople, they can disagree, and a conversation about numbers can grow passionate. Giving the board governing powers increases that passion, the Network has found. "If a board is only 'advisory,' our experience shows that the board members are not invested and do not assist in getting jobs for students and donations for schools or contribute time to the degree that a 'governing' board does," a "lessons learned" document reads.[13]

In this case, the Cristo Rey Boston board compromised, cutting the budget some, but also doing a better job raising money and collecting work-study revenues to prevent a cash shortage. "I love the fact that it's a school without a lot of money, and what money we do utilize we utilize dearly and very effectively," says board member Hugh McLaughlin, executive vice president of business development at Sullivan & McLaughlin, a family construction company.

Still Religious

Kendall, Thielman's old colleague from the Chicago school and the Network, also took over a struggling school. Kendall became president of Cristo Rey St. Martin College Prep in Waukegan, Illinois, in 2011. Waukegan sits about forty-five miles north of Chicago and just ten miles south of the Wisconsin border. Though the school is just blocks from Lake Michigan, Waukegan is better known for its lakefront manufacturing plants than the natural beauty or towering skyline of its neighbors. When those plants started closing down in the 1970s, Waukegan lost much of its wealth.

Waukegan's Cristo Rey school opened in 2004, started by a lay board led by Father George J. Rassas, now an auxiliary bishop for the Archdiocese of Chicago. Waukegan is one of the schools in the Cristo Rey Network that has no religious sponsors. Instead, three religious communities endorse the school: the Clerics of St. Viator and two orders of women religious, the Sinsinawa Dominicans and the Society of the Holy Child Jesus. While religious sponsors ensure the financial viability of the school, assist with staffing the school, and reserve powers such as approval of the school president, an endorsement simply ensures the Catholicity of the school. Cristo Rey St. Martin gives each of the endorsing communities a spot on the board, which the Viatorians filled with a layman. Though there are no financial requirements to endorse a school, Kendall says the three religious orders have been generous.

Lay leadership brings the strong knowledge of and connections to the business community that Foley desired when he hired Kendall and Thielman. Still, Kendall notes that it is hard to match the connections that the Jesuits provide for the original school in Chicago. The Jesuits sponsor eight and endorse three of the twenty-eight Cristo Rey Network schools open in 2014. With a long tradition of running high schools and colleges, the Jesuits can tap into the philanthropic and higher-education communities when opening a new high school. They also have a wide network of successful alumni educated to be "men and women for others," and they are often eager to help their former teachers with jobs and donations. Both Kendall and Foley, for instance, are graduates of Loyola Academy, a prestigious Jesuit college-prep school in the northern suburbs of Chicago. One decided to join the Jesuits and the other went to work and had a family, but both share the same values.

THE JESUIT CONNECTION

Bob Dunn, the founding board chair of Cristo Rey Jesuit College Preparatory School in Houston, first learned about the Cristo Rey model through a former teacher at his alma mater, Strake Jesuit College Preparatory. When he learned that the New Orleans province of Jesuits was interested in opening a school in the South, he called his friend and fellow Strake Jesuit alum Brian Branda.

"When Bob first described it to me, it took about five seconds to go, 'What a great idea,'" recalls Branda, who followed Dunn as board chair. It made sense to them both as people of faith and as businesspeople. The two gathered about fifteen laypeople, mostly businesspeople connected to Strake Jesuit, to form a feasibility committee. "One of the reasons our board has been so success- ful is because it's largely businesspeople," posits Dunn. "Everyone who gets involved has taken ownership. It's amazing how people have answered the call."

Some have gotten involved because they see themselves in the students. Board member Lupe Fraga, for instance, owns a suc- cessful independent office supply store, Tejas Office Products, Inc. He grew up in the poor east end of Houston and credits an ath- letic scholarship to a Catholic high school for changing his life. Other board members came from wealthy backgrounds that al- lowed them to attend the elite Strake Jesuit. "Selfishly, it's an op- portunity to become involved in a project that could really change somebody's life," Branda says.

The board works with President Father T. J. Martinez, SJ, a young priest whose charisma and enthusiasm for Cristo Rey rivals Foley's, to lead the school. Whether giving a pep talk to stu- dents or donors, Martinez wears his signature Texas belt buckle, cowboy boots, and wide, open-mouthed grin with his black cler- ics. Though he and the board have raised more than $20 million for the school, Martinez came into the job with no experience running an organization. He had spent the entirety of his adult life in school—first college, then law school, and then years of seminary and postgraduate work in education as part of his Jesuit formation. His lack of expertise led him to rely on laypeople on his board and in the school.

"Not having any long-term experience in running an educational institution turned out to be a huge benefit," Martinez explains. "I didn't know what I couldn't do. When I founded Cristo Rey Jesuit, I wanted to use a corporate leadership model rather than an educational one. The traditional, hierarchical approach to high schools where the president and principal make all the decisions I found inefficient, disempowering, and ineffective."

Martinez put into place "a corporate, collaborative, team approach," as he describes it. The President's Cabinet, as he named his team, includes the principal, corporate work-study director, and development director—three positions that each school is required to have—as well as a director of technology, a director of admissions, and a director of finance, facilities, and human resources. "Each school leader takes charge—and ownership—of the different facets of the school, while also being commonly responsible for the mission at large," Martinez says. "The principal does not have to worry if the lights do not go on in the kitchen. Everyone is able to maximize and focus their skill set to run Cristo Rey Jesuit as well as push for the success of the entire mission, allowing the school to become the fastest-growing school in the history of the Network."

Martinez converted the old boys' locker room into the school's central office, calling it "the bullpen." He put himself in the cage where football uniforms used to be stored. Instead of putting up a wall, he retained the original metal grating, which keeps his office open to his Cabinet. Where lockers and benches once stood, office desks face each other in a semicircle with a conference table in the middle of the room to promote collaboration. Martinez rarely has had to dictate the direction of the school. Every major decision that affects the entire school is made by all of those directors, he says. Martinez hopes that his collaborative approach to school leadership will help institutionalize its culture and processes, rather than letting the school rely on any one leader's personality, however strong his own may be.

When Martinez went to Africa as part of his tertianship, the final stage of his formation as a Jesuit, corporate work-study director Dan Walsh stepped in as interim president. The "special magic" that Martinez brings to catalyzing the wider community around the school's mission cannot be replaced, Walsh says. Walsh focused more of his energies internally on school operations than Martinez did, but this shift was driven more by the momentum and stage of the school, entering maturity in its fifth year, than his own personality. "I'm not going to turn the place upside down, and quite frankly it doesn't need it," he said during the middle of his interim presidency.

The model of leadership that Martinez instituted allowed his temporary leave to be relatively seamless. It works because spreading leadership requires that all the director roles be filled with "top-caliber talent," Walsh explains. Although each person may have a different leadership style and personality, he says, they share Martinez's "contagious enthusiasm" for the mission as a whole.

Teachers as Learners

The environment that Kauffmann sought as a teacher after one year in a public school is rooted in the philosophy of the original

Cristo Rey school in Chicago. When she recruited the first team of Cristo Rey teachers, principal Sister Judy Murphy, OSB, established an innovative student-centered education, asking her teachers to look at their students' unique challenges and come up with a curriculum that would work for them.[14]

Murphy insisted on keeping the school small and providing teachers with common planning time in order to allow teachers to work together on their student-centered curriculum. They would teach in teams, compare notes about students, and share ideas. Even the physical setting of the first school lent itself to collaboration. When the school opened, teachers' desks were tucked into a windowless basement storage room out of a lack of space. When the school planned a new building, teachers wanted to keep their communal space, so two classrooms were reserved as a faculty office.[15]

"In a lot of schools, you have your own room," Julie Minikel-Lacocque, one of the first teachers, explains in *More Than a Dream,* a book that chronicles the beginning of Cristo Rey Jesuit in Chicago. "You eat lunch in your room. You go to your room during your free period and grade papers. But we all had our desks in that one small room. It forced us to share the space and ideas."[16]

Such an environment does not come naturally to some schools. Before Kauffmann arrived at Cristo Rey Boston, each classroom was in its own silo. Teachers worked independently, and taught their own curriculums. When teachers tried to get together and improve the school, they ran into an unreceptive administration. Establishing an effective learning community requires both willing teachers and strong instructional leadership from a principal. Thanks to lessons learned during the Network's first years, Cristo Rey schools across the country have reformed their academic departments.

Dan O'Connell, principal of Verbum Dei High School in Los Angeles, the only all-boys Cristo Rey school, is emblematic of this new generation of academic leaders. As a young principal, O'Connell was eager to take advantage of the Network resources when he started working at Verbum Dei in 2008. In 2009, he jumped at the opportunity to be a part of a Network-wide initiative to develop and test a common curriculum, improve instruction, and help principals become stronger leaders.

O'Connell came to Verbum Dei because he believes in education's ability to change lives. The Cristo Rey model, he knew, would allow him to provide the same world-class education that he enjoyed growing up in LA to low-income students. In a neighborhood that is 99 percent Latino and African-American, O'Connell's pale pink skin, red hair, and goatee make him stick out.[17] But like many of the Latino families at Verbum Dei, his great-grandparents were immigrants who had nothing when they came to the United States. They believed in education and sacrificed to send their children to Catholic schools, he says. His great-uncles ended up a dentist and a doctor, but O'Connell particularly marvels at his grandmother. As a woman in the 1930s, she earned a master's degree in education from Columbia University. "In one generation, they went from dirt poor, living in a poor, immigrant neighborhood in the Bronx, to having this education," he says. "It transforms families."

Two generations later, O'Connell attended Loyola High School, Los Angeles's "traditional affluent Jesuit high school," as O'Connell describes it. "I credit that school with making me who I am," he says. Educated to be a "man for others," O'Connell asked himself how he could make a difference in the world. He found his answer in education. After college, he went back to work for his high-school alma mater, but he was not satisfied.

"Every kid in the United States should have the opportunity to have this type of education," he thought. While teaching at Loyola, he earned a master's degree and doctorate in educational leadership for social justice at Loyola Marymount University, where he studied how to lead a school for the underserved—a school like Verbum Dei. The mission of the Cristo Rey–model school mirrors O'Connell's personal mission.

When he greets a new class of students on their first day of school, O'Connell reassures a quiet room full of fourteen-year-old boys in crisp white dress shirts and black ties that they belong at the school. "We believe you have what it takes to succeed here," he says, telling them how special they are for showing up at school in the middle of the summer to go through work-study training. Their dedication will help them get to college. "But we need you to step it up," he adds. He shares a favorite analogy for the school—a staircase that you have to climb rather than an elevator that does all the work for you. Students are not on that staircase alone, though. O'Connell asks the boys to look at their neighbors. "Today, they become your brothers," he says.

O'Connell will come to learn the names of each freshman at

the school. As he walks through the open-air campus, he greets students and adults with equal respect, stopping for short conversations.

O'Connell roots his work in the Ignatian ideals of *cura personalis* and *magis*—care for the entire person and doing more. These qualities run strong both at the Jesuit-run Verbum Dei and all Cristo Rey schools. Teachers and administrators ask a lot of the students while providing a safe, caring environment.

O'Connell makes time to speak on the students' first day of school and at the ceremony in the spring of their senior year when they announce their college decisions. He sits in the audience of school plays, laughing along with the students when one of the boys plays a female part. Still, his job takes him off campus more than most Cristo Rey principals. Because Verbum Dei is a part of the archdiocese, the Jesuit Secondary Education Association, and the Cristo Rey Network, O'Connell is often away at meetings or in his office trying to figure out how to prioritize the organizations' various requirements.

For instance, the Cristo Rey Network encourages principals to get into each teacher's classroom once a week. Principals are to be "leaders of learning" rather than the "principal-managers" of yesterday, as Elizabeth Goettl, who served as chief academic officer for the Cristo Rey Network from 2009 to 2014, says. In Cristo Rey classrooms across the Network, students hardly flinch when a visitor enters the classroom.

O'Connell embraces this idea—when he is able to. When he is on campus, O'Connell is analyzing data, working with teachers to set goals, and observing classrooms. "Sometimes I think my teachers think I'm a pain in the butt, but I'm always constantly trying to figure out how can we do things better," he says.

Because of his outside responsibilities, O'Connell also empowers his teachers to be leaders. He has an assistant principal who focuses on academics and department chairs who help with classroom evaluations. Other Cristo Rey schools split academic leadership between deans. Schools frequently require teachers to observe each other and discuss teaching strategies and student learning. Regardless of the organization, Cristo Rey principals generally agree with O'Connell's attitude. "I'm the instructional leader here, but it doesn't mean that it's all me," he says. "Why have these great people working here, if I'm the only one getting in there and giving recommendations on instruction?"

Verbum Dei's math department works together all the time, teacher Jessica Strains says. If they teach different sections of the same class, teachers will create lectures, quizzes, and practice problems together. Students have textbooks that they keep at home as a reference, but the practice problems are too basic and do not require students to make connections, so teachers create their own homework problems. "I think our quality of material goes up, and also it helps the production. We do a lot of divide and conquer," Strains says. "It's also a nice way for us to get together and say, 'Your students seemed to do a lot better than my students did on this learning target. Can you let me know what you might have done differently?' It's a way for us to use best practices too."

When she and fellow math teacher Sarah Myers compared notes about their freshman Algebra I class at Verbum Dei, for instance, they found they were dealing with the same struggle.

Each had unusually small classes of only ten students, but the students were at a wide variety of levels. It is a common problem. On the one hand, it is easier to teach students in classrooms where all are at the same level, but, on the other hand, students who are behind can benefit from being in the same classroom with higher-achieving students.

They approached the math department chair with a proposal to combine classes. The school gave them the flexibility to try it out, and the experiment worked well. In one class session, Strains went through a problem, while Myers circulated around the room, answering individual questions and encouraging boys to take notes. When they assigned practice problems, Strains took a group of five students who were still struggling with the concept to a table in the back of the classroom for further explanation, while Myers supervised the larger group working on a practice problem set that ranged from "basic" to "challenge" questions.

Although the team-taught Algebra I classroom might have been unique in the Cristo Rey Network, the commitment to problem solving is consistent across schools, Goettl says. "There's this culture of continuous improvement, because until we achieve the results we want to achieve from our students, we haven't arrived. We need to continue to ask, 'What can we do differently as the adults in this school to achieve the results we want to get from our students?'"

Furthermore, as Kauffmann learned at the Boston public school, this mentality cannot exist in only one classroom. "Kids learn best if they have a whole school of effective teachers, and that only happens if the principal hires the right teachers, trains them, and holds them accountable," Goettl says.

The idea seems reasonable, but Bryk, Lee, and Holland in *Catholic Schools and the Common Good* confirmed it to be true. Higher incidences of staffing problems were associated with students being less oriented to academics and sophomore achievement being lower, while a stable teaching force was associated with higher achievement.[18] This is both a strength and a challenge for Cristo Rey schools—principals must find teachers who believe wholeheartedly in the mission of the school, are willing to constantly challenge themselves to do better for their students, and are willing to accept pay that is often under the market rate for public-school teachers.

Myers and Strains do not look like what you might expect of math teachers. Strains clicks around the classroom in fashionable shoes and a hip blouse and pants; her hair is held back in a ponytail and she wears a black headband with a bow. Myers has long blond hair and big caring eyes. She is the type of teacher who notices when boys come in with a new haircut, and it makes them feel special. Myers wears a professional-looking skirt and heels and a large diamond on her ring finger.

Myers came to Verbum Dei after a three-month stint as a substitute math teacher at a public school in a wealthy beach community in Los Angeles County. Like Kauffmann, she was discouraged by her experience at the public school, though for different reasons. She had about thirty-six students in each class, and there was a constant push to move forward. "If anyone needed help, there really wasn't any time to help them. I was forced to move on," she says. "There was something in my heart that said this wasn't right."

Myers had spent a few years after college figuring out that she wanted to teach and then earning her credential. But her public-school experience made her want to quit teaching entirely. "I had finally realized what I wanted to do, but when I did it, I just felt empty," she says. "I hated going to work. I never wanted to teach again. I thought I was not cut out for teaching. When you're in that position, it's really hard to say, 'It's not me; it's the situation.'"

Myers applied for forty or fifty nonteaching jobs after her experience as a substitute teacher. When she saw the Verbum Dei job, though, she got excited by the idea of teaching again. "For the first time in a long time, my heart was beating fast while I was reading the job description. It just felt right," she says.

While subbing, Myers could not pinpoint what was missing at the public school. She only realized what it was later. "I was missing the faith," says Myers, whose single mother, a waitress, supported her through Catholic high school. "I was missing the small connections that you make; I was missing the care and love."

Working at Verbum Dei required that she take an $8,000 cut in annual pay, but the decision to accept the job was not difficult. "No money in the world is worth being in a position you don't like and are not passionate about," Myers says. "I tell my students I'm rich in smiles, because I'm rewarded by way more than money."

For Strains, it is the love of teaching that brought her to the school. Strains found Verbum Dei when she was looking for a job in Los Angeles, so that she could be in the same city as her now husband. In her student teaching, she had taught both low- and high-income students—calculus and remedial algebra. She most enjoyed working with the students who were behind—who were also the ones coming from low-income communities. "You don't expect it anymore," she says. "You think everybody's given a fair chance, but they're not." Though nervous about the prospect of teaching only boys, she was excited to find a job teaching low-income students at Verbum Dei, eager to apply what she had learned as a math, German, and secondary education major.

"I think the reason I really like teaching students that start off behind is that they don't even know their potential yet," Strains explains. "I love seeing them have those moments when they realize that this is something they can be good at."

Helping them reach these moments requires a great deal of effort. Both Myers and Strains start work at 6:45 A.M. and tutor students between 7:00 and 7:30. At that time in the morning, Strains says, at least her commute to Watts is only half an hour. Teachers have office hours after school, sticking around until at least 4:00. Strains sits in traffic for fifty minutes to get home. Myers likes to stay later, but both also say they work at home in the evening and on the weekends, grading papers or looking for new ways to excite students about learning.

Right now, the schedule is demanding, but manageable, Strains says, but she cannot imagine how her coworkers with kids do it. Both she and Myers want to have children someday. Day care, Myers points out, may cost as much as her monthly salary. Strains says that she and her husband will have to reevaluate their budget when they decide to start a family. Catholic school pay is fine for a dual-income couple without kids in Los Angeles, but it would be difficult to start a family at her and her husband's current salaries.

O'Connell empathizes with the struggle he sees his young teachers go through. "I'd love to pay these teachers a million dollars," O'Connell says. Median salaries at Verbum Dei range from $42,000 for a first-year teacher to $48,000 for a tenth-year teacher, which is about average for the Network, but well below the $65,500 median salary of a public-school teacher in Los Angeles.[19]

Young teachers come to Cristo Rey schools with a passion for the mission, O'Connell says, but after a few years, he sees them struggle with the reality that, with their income, they may never be able to buy a home or support a family in Los Angeles. The fair market rate to rent an apartment—the amount paid by Section 8 voucher holders—is about $1,100 for a one-bedroom apartment. To afford an apartment at this fair market rate, an individual needs to earn $44,000 a year, based on spending one-third of one's income on housing.[20] The average Verbum Dei teacher, therefore, can only afford to rent a fair-market-rate one-bedroom apartment, while the average rent in Los Angeles can be hundreds more.[21]

"On our salary scale, if you have a few kids in your household, your kids would qualify to go to the school," O'Connell says. He knows many Catholic school teachers who must send their own kids to public schools. "There's something inherently wrong with that. At the same time, there are constraints with our budget."

Teacher pay is an issue at most Cristo Rey schools, though it is hard to compare salaries across the Network. In Houston, Cristo Rey Jesuit's tremendous fund-raising success allows the school to be competitive with both local Catholic and public schools, which have the same salary scales. It is on its way to matching this salary scale. Cristo Rey Jesuit's range of salaries is nearly the same as

Verbum Dei's salaries, and yet Houston has a much lower cost of living.[22]

Christ the King Preparatory School in Newark, in contrast, sits in an expensive metropolitan area. Even for teachers with ten years' experience, the median salary of $36,000 is less than other local Catholic schools' median salary.[23] One young teacher who got married in the summer of 2013 left for another Catholic prep school because he could not afford to keep working at Christ the King.

Cristo Rey teachers tend to be young—and without major financial obligations. About half of teachers in the Network have fewer than five years of experience.[24] But budget is not the only reason Cristo Rey attracts young teachers. They also generally have the energy and enthusiasm for the work of inner-city education, and because they have little experience, they are open to training and new ideas about education. Though it is not universally true, principals report that more experienced teachers sometimes do not last at Cristo Rey schools because they cannot get used to the open-door policy in classrooms and the constant push to improve instruction.

"When a school fails, it's because of the lack of learning among the adults," says Weitzel-O'Neill of Boston College. "Of all the professions, the one that should be most anxious to continue learning would be educators."

Kauffmann calls himself one of the "elder statesmen" of Cristo Rey Boston. He has taught for four years at Cristo Rey Boston and seven years total, including his volunteer years at the Chicago school. Young teachers go into urban education because their lives allow for it and they have the energy and desire to do so, but they stay for a different reason, he says. "I love it because it's a challenge. I didn't want a job that would end at 5:00. I wanted something that would always give me something to go home and continue thinking about."

Kauffmann has hope that the young set of teachers who have joined the school since he began will stay too. The qualities of adaptability and desire are more about attitude than age, he says. The desire to keep learning, for instance, motivates a science teacher who is years older than Kauffmann to stay at Cristo Rey Boston while others leave, Kauffmann says with admiration.

Teachers at the Boston school and other Cristo Rey schools have systems where teachers can observe and learn from each other. Teacher-led professional development is a best practice, says Andrew Hoyt, the founding English teacher at Cristo Rey Jesuit in Houston. Hoyt has since returned to graduate school at the University of Notre Dame to study professional development for teachers. At the Houston school, two teachers are named peer leaders and coordinate a system of classroom observations likened to rounds in a hospital. Teachers observe each other, debriefing after the class. The administrative team is not involved, and the discussion is not evaluative. "The idea is just to get you to think about your own practice, not say this person is a good teacher or this person is a bad teacher," Hoyt explains. It allows teachers to "steal" instructional strategies. "I think Cristo Rey schools, especially the start-ups, attract a certain personality, people who are itching to dive in and create that kind of experiential learning, to have this sort of adventure," he says.

Back at Verbum Dei in Los Angeles, John Stradley uses many of the same teaching tools in his freshman-year writing class that Kauffmann uses in his English classes. Like Kauffmann, he is a white, bearded, male English teacher with a love for the profession of teaching. Stradley came to Verbum Dei in 2008 from an affluent Catholic middle school, where he had been teaching for ten years. He liked the idea of working with older students, though he quickly found out that he would have to teach the freshman students the same skills that he taught at the middle school.

"This job is a joy for me," he says. "There are days when it's not particularly joyous, but I really do love teaching. I love seeing students succeed. I love watching them go from students who cannot string a thought together in writing to being college-ready seniors. How many careers do you have where you get to see a transformation take place in three or four years?"

The school's administration has relied on Stradley to teach one of its most essential classes, the "double dose" writing class. Freshmen take another period of English, but Stradley's writing class gets them up to speed and lays the groundwork for the rest of their high-school education. When Network leaders saw the rise in English test scores coming out of Verbum Dei, they flew Stradley to a national conference. Along with a teacher from the Tucson school, which also has a double dose of English for freshmen, Stradley shared what he was doing with the presidents and principals. Now double-dosing is common across the Network.

In Los Angeles's cool morning air—which would have Cristo Rey Boston students sweating in pants and ties—Stradley stands in front of a classroom of freshman boys, wearing an Indiana Jones–

like leather jacket and black dress pants. "Mr. Rios," he calls out, asking a student at the front of the class to read a line of poetry from a worksheet and identify the prepositional phrase. Through Network professional development sessions in the summer, Stradley has picked up new ways to make sure that his students are mastering the material. It has been hard to get used to not calling on students who raise their hands, he says, but he now relies on cold-calling in his classroom. As a teacher, you know the students who raise their hands understand the concept, he says. It is the other students he worries about.

"How does the fog sit, Mr. Woods?" Stradley asks another boy slouching in his own fog in the back row. Stradley walks to the back of the room and stands next to him.

"Silent?" Derek Woods answers uncertainly.

Instead of moving on, Stradley implements the "no opt out" teaching strategy, trying to help Derek recognize the part of speech. "Is that a descriptive word?"

Derek squirms. "I don't know."

Stradley explains that it is an adjective, and they are looking for the prepositional phrase.

Derek looks down at his paper. "I don't get it."

Stradley returns to Mr. Rios to help him out. "On silent haunches," Miguel Rios responds from the front of the room.

But Stradley has not given up on Derek. "There was a reason you weren't able to answer any of those. It's because you didn't do the homework," he tells the boy quietly, urging him to come in after school.

These are the less "joyous" moments of his work, but in a

school survey students said that the teachers who badger them to seek help and do better are the ones who really care. Stradley, therefore, has redoubled his efforts to reach out to struggling students.

Though he has been teaching prepositions for years, Stradley decided to try something new this year to show students how to apply the grammar lesson. He played the first few minutes of *Indiana Jones,* asking the students to write down prepositional phrases to describe the action. Though they were disappointed when he turned the movie off, they were also eager to share their examples of Indiana Jones going *into* the cave and *through* various traps. Stradley lives for moments of creativity in lesson planning and moments of discovery by students—the "aha!" moments.

In the middle of the spring 2013 semester, Stradley took the time to think about his values as an educator and write them out before a teacher's meeting. It was not part of professional development or a class. "It just came upon me that I wanted to formulate what it is that is important to me," he says. He shared them with other teachers and keeps them posted in his classroom. "Real growth involves commitment, diligence, hard work, and genuine effort," reads the second value on the list. The value applies to students and teachers alike at Cristo Rey schools.

An Employment Agency Within a School

Had Preston Kendall not found Cristo Rey, he might have been like Stradley or Kauffmann. Instead, he found a position in which he was able to combine his desire to educate with his business expertise. As the first work-study director of the original Cristo Rey school, he became the archetypal person to fill a difficult role.

Kendall majored in English at Northwestern University and had considered teaching. But he and his high-school sweetheart, Ginny, married and started a family young, and Kendall felt a responsibility to provide for his new family. He went to business school at Northwestern's Kellogg School of Management and rose up through the ranks to vice president of an insurance company started by his great-grandfather—it had gone public and was no longer owned by the family.

With a broad frame, balding hair, and skin that reddens with excitement, Kendall looks as though he belongs in a corner office. He comes to life drawing graphs on a whiteboard in a conference room. But in the mid-1990s, there was no room for advancement at the insurance company. His superiors were not much older than he was and planned to stay at the company for a long time.

Two deaths also made him think twice about his career direction. A coworker, Joseph Begny, died in a plane crash on a flight that Kendall had frequently taken with him. The company did not plan to send anybody to the funeral, so Kendall used his vacation time to attend. "I just couldn't believe the way Joe's death was handled. At that point, I said, 'I've gotta get out of this,' " he recalled in *More Than a Dream*.[25]

He also had the chance to talk with his grandfather before he died in hospice, and his grandfather shared his regrets about giving up the family business. "You know, Preston," Kendall recalls his grandfather saying, "when I get up to heaven, my dad's going to kick my butt."

Kendall did not want to have those regrets. "I don't want to feel that when everything's over, somebody's going to kick my butt," he says.

Kendall interviewed for other jobs, but everything he looked at was basically the same job with a different name on the front door, he says. In the back of his mind was a mission trip to Peru that he had taken between his sophomore and junior years at Loyola Academy. "Peru really rocked my world," he says. "They say that if you work for the poor, they will evangelize you."

With Ginny's encouragement, Kendall considered going into education. He visited the central offices for a wealthy North Suburban school district to find out how to become an accredited teacher, but he came away disappointed. "It looks like I'm going to have to throw away all my business background and start over," he told Ginny.

But within a few days, Ginny was calling him on a pay phone from the train station to tell him to check out the *Chicago Sun-Times*. There was an article about a new Jesuit high school with a work program that seemed perfect for him, she said.[26]

What is more, Father John Foley was part of the team opening the school. Kendall had met Foley, a fellow Loyola Academy grad, on that trip to Peru. They had even stood next to each other, Foley's arm around Kendall, in a picture of the group after a Mass at Machu Picchu. Kendall quickly wrote a letter to Foley saying that he wanted to help the new school. Though it had been more than fifteen years, Foley remembered him right away. He called and invited Kendall to visit Pilsen, where he explained to Kendall that he was looking for a businessperson to run the work program. After that visit, Kendall knew that he had found what he was looking for. "I felt very, very strongly that I was made for that position," he says.

Like Kendall, many of the work-study directors at the Cristo Rey schools say that providence—or the Holy Spirit—brought them to the school. Dan Walsh, a Kellogg School of Management graduate like Kendall and the founding corporate work-study director at Cristo Rey Houston, quit his job at the Coca-Cola Company looking for something more—at the start of the economic recession. "I knew there was a greater good out there, and I didn't know what it was," Walsh says. "Friends and family members thought I was totally crazy."

The death of his grandmother caused him to reevaluate how he was spending his life. "I come from a can-do family with a tradition of improving themselves and serving others along the way," he says. "I've always had in my head and my heart a zeal for business and entrepreneurship, yet simultaneously a real passion and calling to serve and have an enduring impact long after I'm gone from this earth."

Walsh did some consulting and dipped into his savings to stay afloat while figuring out what he wanted to do with his career. After a fellow University of Notre Dame alum shared a 2004 *60 Minutes* story on Cristo Rey with him, he immediately decided to start volunteering at the Houston school, which was gearing up to open. After Walsh worked on a committee charged with developing the work-study training program, Martinez, the school presi-

dent, offered him the job of corporate work-study director just three
weeks before the first freshmen were to start the training program.

The offer brought Walsh full circle to his college graduation,
when he was uncertain whether to follow his passion for business or service. At the time, he had asked Father Theodore M.
Hesburgh, CSC, for advice, and the legendary president of Notre
Dame had talked with him about his future for an hour in his
stately office, with the crest of Notre Dame on the carpet and
a view of the famed golden dome out the window. "Somehow,
someday, you'll find your way," Hesburgh had told him. With
Cristo Rey, Walsh finally had.

Still, with each providential story come challenges. Kendall had
to make up the position as he went along, and he soon found out
that it was much more work than he could handle alone. Outside
the Cristo Rey Network schools, there is no equivalent position. Pay
is competitive, but the businesspeople the schools are looking for
could certainly make more in industry. At each Network gathering
of corporate work-study directors, there are many new faces due to
high turnover. Like Kendall and Walsh, though, those who have
found the most success and satisfaction from the position combine
business experience with a passion for education and service.

Work-study directors run a separate nonprofit placement service within the context of a high school. It is essentially a temporary employment agency. As in any business, the director's role is
to sell a product and keep customers satisfied, but in this unique
situation the work-study program's clients are corporate sponsors
and its products are the student workers.

Sales experience comes in handy for the corporate work-study director's number-one responsibility: finding jobs for students. Working off introductions from board members and friends of the school, the director attempts to persuade CEOs to become corporate sponsors, selling the student workers as reliable, low-cost, entry-level labor with great promise for their futures. They also appeal to the CEO's belief in developing a diverse workforce.

The schools' financial model rests on the work-study directors' ability to sell and keep jobs. At full enrollment, more than half of a school's operating budget is designed to come from the work program. The financial model requires that a school meet a certain threshold of enrollment—four to six hundred students bringing in money. When no seats are empty, the money spent on facilities and teachers is being used as efficiently as possible. If there are more students than jobs, the school will have to rely on fund-raising and tuition, neither of which is as sustainable as work-study revenue. Student enrollment, therefore, is limited by the number of jobs that the work-study director can find.

The director needs to find new jobs both to increase enrollment and to replace companies that do not renew. With an average renewal rate of 90 percent, it is relatively rare that companies do not sign on again, but the program can lose renewals due to corporate mergers or shifts in the business climates. Because the contracts are annual, directors must be as attuned to keeping their corporate customers happy as they are to finding new companies to sign up.

Customer service is where the job becomes complicated. The work-study office checks in with supervisors through phone calls and site visits to ensure that companies are happy with the students. But responding to the companies' requests also requires training the students with both the hard and soft skills required in corporate America—everything from using Excel to making small talk. Students go through training during the summer before their freshman year.

Finally, there is the logistical side to the job. The corporate work-study office takes care of tax and legal forms required to allow minors to work. Before it sends anyone to work, the school has to confirm that students meet age and immigration-status work requirements.

The office also must transport and keep track of the 25 percent of the student body that leaves campus on any given day. Kendall tells a story from the first year of the Cristo Rey program in *More Than a Dream*. At the time, Kendall was not only work-study director, but also a bus driver. When he went downtown to pick up the students from work on one rainy day that first fall, he could not find one student. After taking the other student workers back to school and returning downtown to search for him, he finally got the boy's phone number and called his home. The boy had taken public transportation home rather than wait in the rain.

Another student, Kendall says, had been getting off the bus downtown, but not showing up at work. He was uncomfortable with the work, but too scared to tell anybody, so he spent his days wandering around downtown Chicago instead of working. Months passed before the school and corporate sponsor put two and two together. Kendall and his associate started calling sponsors every morning to make sure students had made it to work.

They soon created a paper sign-in sheet—students had to have their supervisors sign it to confirm students were at work.[27]

The responsibilities of the corporate work-study office can be overwhelming, because at stake is not only the school's financial sustainability, but also the students' well-being. To meet this wide variety of duties, the typical corporate work-study office now has four full-time equivalent employees.[28]

Laura Capasso worked in the Cristo Rey Boston work-study office through the AmeriCorps volunteer program during the 2012–13 school year. Each morning, she would set up a podium at the door of an empty classroom and place the list of students who were working that day. Students lined up at the door in coats and sweatshirts, earphones ready for their morning commute.

"Where's your tie?" asked Capasso, herself dressed for corporate America in a silk blouse, black pencil skirt, and heels, with a simple cross around her neck. She leaned over the podium to inspect the student's outfit. The Boston school does not have a uniform, simply a professional dress code.

Once through their inspection, students sat in the desks, waiting to hear the school announcements. Some picked up a brown-bag lunch from a tray sitting to the side of the room. The lunch contained a calzone, apple, bag of chips, and juice. A work supervisor had called in recently, concerned that her student worker was not eating anything for lunch, and the school chef responded by offering to-go lunches for all students. Most students rely on free or reduced-price lunches at the school, but at work they have to take care of themselves.

There is a subway stop across the street from the school. After being dismissed, most students take the train downtown to work and are on their own for the rest of the day. Some are driven in vans.

Boston has implemented an online system where both students and supervisor sign in and write a few lines about the day's work. For most of the year, though, Capasso would bundle up for the Boston winter and take her clipboard out to a central downtown subway stop where students came to check out with her. Now, reliable workers only have to fill out their timecard online and head directly home, while those who had yet to earn the adults' trust had to come back to the school to check out in person.

In Los Angeles, Cristina Cuellar-Villanueva has slightly more control of the students' comings and goings. After attendance and announcements, Ms. V., as students call her, gives the students a pep talk, reminding them that end-of-the-year reviews are coming, before dismissing the boys by van.

With poor public transportation and jobs in all directions of LA County, the school relies on a fleet of vans and one large bus to get the student workers to their companies and back to school. In addition to the usual responsibilities, she and her work-study staff have to fill their fleet's tanks a few times each week. The work-study program's transportation budget is significant, Cuellar-Villanueva says.

She hires drivers from the local community who are retired or have flexible work schedules. They drive up to two hours round-trip, morning and evening, with the students, and as an added benefit they serve as Cuellar-Villanueva's eyes and ears. Students sometimes will tell the drivers more about work than they do the work-study staff. A driver may notice that a student is always sleeping in the van, hinting that something might be keeping him from resting well at home.

Although it is her job to keep an eye on the students, Cuellar-Villanueva does not have to worry about finding new jobs as director of operations. She leaves that to her partner Larry Scott, vice president of corporate recruitment. When she and Scott started at the school in 2004, their supervisor was in charge of both the day-to-day operations and the sales function. When the supervisor left the next year, the two decided to split the leadership role. It is rare to find somebody with the same ability to negotiate with businesspeople as with teens.

Cuellar-Villanueva is a tall, thin Latina with long, dark hair. Having grown up in Watts, she commands students' respect and knows the struggles that they and their families face on a daily basis. But, being from the neighborhood, Cuellar-Villanueva did not think highly of Verbum Dei before she started working there. Verbum Dei had been on the brink of closure when the Jesuits took over and converted the school to the Cristo Rey model, but even in its first years as a Cristo Rey school it struggled to adapt to the new model of education.

As a student at Loyola Marymount University, Cuellar-Villanueva worked with a Verbum Dei student worker at the Center of Service and Action. She was not impressed. "He'd walk in with this headphones and a hooded sweatshirt. It just seemed to me like he was wasting time," she remembers. She balked when her boss at the center told her about an opening for a work-study program coordinator at Verbum Dei.

But as a Spanish major who had taken a few education classes, she wanted to find a career involving service. She overcame her prejudices and applied for the position. "The minute I walked on this campus, I fell in love with it," she says. The energy and mission of the school excited her. She just had to start enforcing rules—such as no headphones at work—that others had let slip.

By her second semester on campus, she started hearing the same question from all her students, over and over again: "Hey, Ms. V., are you coming back next year?" At first she thought the question odd, but then she began to understand—turnover at the school had been so bad that students did not trust that anyone would be there for them the next year. She saw that this culture was at the root of students' misbehavior and lack of effort. "Why would the students and families care? 'You're not committed to me, why would I be committed to you?'" Cuellar-Villanueva says.

It is not enough to have consistency in the classroom or a businessperson in the work-study office; all of the workers at the school, from teachers to work-study bus drivers, have to get behind the students and push them forward. Today, Verbum Dei has overcome the negative reputation it had prior to becoming a Cristo Rey school when she was growing up in Watts, Cuellar-Villanueva says. The students want to come to "the Verb," as they know the school. They want to go to work, and they know they will have support.

"I don't get that question anymore. They're not asking, 'Hey, are you coming back?'" Cuellar-Villanueva says. "In a community that's plagued with inconsistencies and lack of resources and letdowns, Verbum Dei has to work its magic to lift them up."

The Gift of Volunteers

By second semester of her volunteer year at Cristo Rey Boston, Laura Capasso was the person with the longest tenure in the Cristo Rey Boston corporate work-study office. The difficulty of the work had led to unusually high turnover during the first semester. Although people throughout the school tried to help, they had their own important jobs to do. Capasso ended up working from 6:30 A.M. to 9:30 P.M.—every day for a good two months, she says. "The majority of my day is putting out fires."

At the same time that Laura was throwing herself into the school as a volunteer, Dave Roberts was tutoring at the school. Having run a boutique staffing firm for years, he also volunteered for the jobs committee, which helps the board generate leads for new work-study sponsors. Roberts was looking for a meaningful way to give back, but board work was not enough for him. He wanted to be on the inside of an organization, helping to solve problems and push growth. A board member suggested he apply for the open corporate work-study director position, and he took over the office during the second semester. As with Kendall, Roberts's business expertise and desire to work with youth made him a perfect fit. "Five minutes with my wife, and she'll tell you I've never been happier," he says with a laugh. "I needed this. Hopefully the school needs me as much as I need this school."

Whether they are spending a year or two after college at Cristo Rey schools or tutoring students after school for an hour or two a week, volunteers enhance the services and support that the schools provide to students. Cristo Rey's mission draws in both those who want to stand in solidarity with the poor and change the world and those who are concerned about the country's workforce. And because the unique model brings together the education and business worlds, there are plenty of opportunities for outsiders to give time and talent.

The original Cristo Rey school in Chicago launched its full-time volunteer program in 1999, just a few years after opening. Other schools tap into organizations such as the Ignatian Volunteer Corps, which allows retirees to volunteer within an organization for two days a week.

In Boston, the AmeriCorps program helps bolster the school's services to students while giving young people the experience of working in an urban Catholic school and potentially finding a career. Volunteers end up getting more out of their year of service than they give, they say.

The volunteers at the Boston school live in an old rectory behind a large stone church a mile away from the school. During the 2012–13 school year, Capasso and her three roommates set their schedules to leave for the school at 7:00 A.M. in one of the work-study minivans. They ate the same breakfast that students were served in the cafeteria.

Capasso and Will Brown, borrowed from the Office of Student Life, headed to the work program's check-in to take attendance and see students off to work. The corporate work-study office is the most common spot for full-time volunteers; nine schools supplement their staff with a volunteer. Cristo Rey Boston also has a volunteer working on admissions.

Cristo Rey Boston places volunteers in nonteaching positions—

teachers must be well-prepared professionals. There are plenty of ways, though, that a volunteer can make a significant contribution to the school. In the Office of Student Life, Brown planned spirit days and retreats and coordinated clubs. He and fellow volunteer Doug McNicol ran a choir, while Rosie Miola, the volunteer in admissions, had a running club. During Cristo Rey Boston's academic and financial turnaround, the school went without a campus minister for a few years, and school spirit suffered without adult leadership. As a volunteer, Brown laid the groundwork for a committee that allows students to take ownership of the school's culture.

Second-year volunteers at the school sometimes get experience in the classroom—with supervision and support. Even outside the classroom, the academic support volunteers provide to students is an important element of the school. In his second year, McNicol taught one section of English while also running the freshman proficiency program, which involves tutoring and monthly tests that ensure freshmen have mastered middle-school skills. After serving in student life, Brown also volunteered for a second year, starting a new program for freshmen most at risk of transferring out of the school. Both programs are designed to give freshmen the foundation they need to succeed at Cristo Rey and beyond.

Volunteers have other miscellaneous—sometimes thankless—assignments, such as swiping cards, serving food, and cleaning up the cafeteria after lunch. Though some volunteers walk home earlier, the volunteer on library duty kicks the last students out at 6:00 P.M., locks up the library for the night, and drives the school van back to the old rectory.

At home, the volunteers share responsibilities for cooking dinner, cleaning, and shopping for groceries. Each is given a $500 monthly stipend, and they decide how much to throw in for shared expenses. The calendar in the kitchen is full of community members' comings and goings, dinner guests, prayer nights, and retreats.

The service combined with the intentional style of life allows the young volunteers to reflect on how they can serve God and neighbor throughout their lives. The volunteers may find a career path, but the program is also a good talent pipeline for the schools, says Kauffmann, the English teacher who started as a volunteer at the Chicago school. He took on the role of volunteer coordinator at Cristo Rey Boston, leading retreats and checking in with the volunteers monthly to make sure they feel comfortable at the school, with their jobs, and in the community.

McNicol found his path through his conversations with Kauffmann. Both men went to St. Joseph University in Philadelphia, and the same professor recommended the Cristo Rey volunteer programs to them. At the time, McNicol thought he wanted to go into elementary education. "I didn't think I was smart enough to be a high-school teacher," he says. Just as going through a Cristo Rey program shows students what they are capable of by raising the bar, volunteering at a Cristo Rey school did the same for him. It both elevated his confidence and gave him a passion for urban education. "I cannot even imagine working with younger kids now," he says.

McNicol followed Kauffmann one step farther by attending Boston College's Donovan Urban Teaching Scholars Program after his volunteer stint. McNicol joined the master's program despite knowing how difficult teaching at a public school was for

Kauffmann. "I encouraged Doug to do it, because it gave me immense perspective," Kauffmann says.

Even though McNicol was excited to start his master's program, he also wanted to stay connected with Cristo Rey. As his volunteer experience came to an end, he was sad that he wouldn't be able to watch the freshmen and sophomores he had worked with grow and develop as people and learners throughout high school.

The students often are disappointed that volunteers move on year after year, but even if they do not say thank you, they do appreciate the effort. As his freshman year nears its end, Stephen Diaz was still working with McNicol on mastering middle-school math. He was hardly thrilled with the sometimes frustrating proficiency program. Yet when asked what he liked about the school, he said the volunteers. "Why would you put up with hardheaded students and put yourself through the stress? Being a teacher is stressful. Why would you do that to yourself and at the end of the day not get paid for it?" Stephen said in a quiet voice. "That person really wants to help people besides themselves."

Chapter Three

From One School to Many: Building a Network of Support

The Cristo Rey Network has twenty-eight schools open and more on their way. As the Network has grown, its annual gatherings have expanded from intimate meetings to full-blown conferences. Today, presidents, principals, corporate work-study directors, board chairs, religious sponsors, and the national office staff come together in hotel ballrooms each spring to share ideas, break bread, and celebrate successes.

In spring 2013, two buses full of school and Network leaders made their way through Minneapolis's still-frozen streets to an airy entrance hall at the University of St. Thomas School of Law, which hosted a banquet for the group. In recent years, the national

Network's board of directors has given out a Founder's Award to someone who has been instrumental to the success of the schools. At the banquet, Father Foley and Father Joseph Parkes, SJ, the former board chair of the Network and president of Cristo Rey New York, took the stage to present the award. When Foley announced his name, Preston Kendall was in disbelief.

The pick did not shock others. Although Kendall was not the one to come up with the work-study model, he did figure out how it would actually work—and made it happen. He also helped Jeff Thielman start the national Network while working at the first school, advising new schools on how to implement the work-study program. He joined the national office when the Network was officially established; then when the second Chicago school started, he returned to the schools to coordinate the two work-study programs. In 2011, when the six-year-old Cristo Rey St. Martin was struggling in Waukegan, he became president of the school and helped it become financially stable.

Trembling with surprise, Kendall approached the platform stage at the banquet to a standing ovation. As he was unprepared, his thanks were brief. Reflecting on the day's sessions, though, he did have one comment to share with all those who run Cristo Rey schools. We keep on pushing students to meet higher standards, Kendall said, "and I ask that we do the same for ourselves."

Belonging to a national network gives member schools both accountability and resources to push themselves to meet higher standards. In addition to replicating the Cristo Rey model in new cities, the primary role of the Network's national offices is to pass on a culture of high expectations with regard to both student academic outcomes and financial sustainability. Kendall wanted to remind his fellow school leaders of this challenge, because throughout the schools' history there has been an ongoing discussion: What does it mean to be a member of a national network, and what does it mean for a school to be a model of education?

In the Beginning

Any uncertainty about the role of the national Cristo Rey Network can be traced back to its beginning. In the fall of 2000, Jeff Thielman, then development director of the lone Cristo Rey Jesuit High School in Chicago, invited an old contact, B. J. Cassin, to visit the school. Cassin was a Silicon Valley venture-capital investor who had benefited from Catholic schooling as a child from a working-class family.[1] He was immediately impressed and wanted to help Cristo Rey. They met with Foley, then school president, and instead of asking for money for the school, as Thielman expected, Foley said they needed to figure out how to replicate the model.[2]

After the visit, Cassin decided to found the Cassin Educational Initiative Foundation with $22 million to replicate the Cristo Rey schools and the NativityMiguel schools, an innovative model of a Catholic middle school serving low-income families. He hired Thielman to run his new foundation. The foundation would fund feasibility studies for new Cristo Rey schools with up to $70,000, provide grants for start-up expenses of new schools, and set up a national network.[3]

The feasibility study was the first step toward institutionalizing the Cristo Rey model. Just as the Jesuits did before they opened the original school, a feasibility committee interviews local leaders, parents, and young people from low-income families. Committee members or religious sponsors have to gather signed letters of intent from companies willing to hire Cristo Rey students and craft a development plan.

As with his business ventures, Cassin wanted to make sure that there was a "market" for each new school. Cristo Rey schools were like investments for him, and he wanted to make sure he was spending his money wisely. It was better to invest $70,000 to run a robust feasibility study than to open a school, only to find out that students would not come or businesses and donors would not support it. Though the feasibility study requirements have been refined, the same general process remains in place today.

At that point, though, the Cristo Rey Network amounted to Thielman spending Cassin's money on starting new schools. Setting up a nonprofit organization to oversee operations was in the five-year plan, but with enthusiasm coming from so many cities interested in opening up Cristo Rey schools, taking the time to do so was not a priority.[4]

Then in December 2002, with schools in Portland, Austin, and Los Angeles already running, Thielman received a call from the Gates Foundation. Tom Vander Ark, the education initiative executive director at the time, had seen a story about the approval of a Cristo Rey school in Denver, his hometown, and he was intrigued.[5] After learning more, he wanted to help Cristo Rey expand, but before the Gates Foundation could donate to the

Cristo Rey Network, the Network had to be formalized. With a $9.9 million grant available, creating a nonprofit structure for the network of schools suddenly became a priority.

Along with incorporation, the Gates Foundation required that there be standards by which it could evaluate the schools. With help from Kendall, Thielman drew up the first draft of the Mission Effectiveness Standards and presented them at a 2003 meeting of school presidents.[6]

The concepts were broad—that the school would be Catholic, only serve the disadvantaged, require a work-study program, and have a college-prep curriculum, to name a few. Even so, they proved controversial. The Mission Effectiveness Standards would have a real impact on the schools. A feasibility committee in New Bern, North Carolina, for example, had seen Cristo Rey as an opportunity to bring a Catholic school to their community. The committee planned for a student body that was only 80 percent "economically disadvantaged," though, so their feasibility study would not be approved.[7]

San Juan Diego Catholic High School in Austin, Texas, which opened as a Cristo Rey school in 2002, decided to leave the Network in 2006 because of this rule. Austin had only one other Catholic high school on the edge of the city at the time, and the bishop believed that he could not deny a Catholic education to Catholics in the diocese if they were not disadvantaged.

Although adding the Mission Effectiveness Standards to the feasibility-study process helped solidify the Cristo Rey model of education, the standards also gave school leaders some flexibility. Schools had the freedom to adapt to local circumstances. With a

diverse student body, the Portland school put less of an emphasis on Spanish language skills in its curriculum than the original school, which serves a Hispanic population. In Los Angeles,
meanwhile, Verbum Dei High School adopted the Cristo Rey
business model at an all-boys school.

But this flexibility also proved challenging. The organizers of
each new school experienced the same frantic push in the year
before opening to find a building, students, corporate sponsors,
staff, and faculty. At the same time, they had to create a curriculum and school culture, policies, and procedures from scratch.[8]
School leaders had to decide how to train students for work, run
campus ministries, and involve and serve parents. Along the way,
they rehashed some of the same debates that leaders of the original school had between academic leaders and those charged with
the school's financial sustainability. Would work get in the way
of academics? How do we form students in a "faith that does
justice" while preparing them to succeed in a sometimes-unjust
economy? How will we raise funds to cover our costs until the
school's work-study program brings in the majority of the budget?
The original school was still struggling with some of these questions after other schools had already opened their doors.

A Change in Strategy

When Rob Birdsell became the president of Cristo Rey Network at
the start of the 2007–08 school year, twelve schools were already operating and seven more schools would open during his first month

on the job. Birdsell, who started his career as a Catholic high-school teacher before going into consulting, inherited a strategic plan called "12 by 12." The Cristo Rey Network wanted to educate twelve thousand students by 2012. With the new schools, Network-wide enrollment jumped from about fourteen hundred students to more than four thousand in the 2007–08 school year. Existing schools would have to grow and multiple new schools be added each year to reach the twelve-thousand-student goal in five years.

Even though it had a strategic plan, the Network was like the "Wild West," Birdsell says. It operated in start-up mode, and in the push to grow, the Network was not paying as much attention to how—and how well—the existing schools were doing their jobs. The biggest challenge Birdsell saw was a lack of structure. Under his tenure, he would build the structures that helped solidify the Cristo Rey model of education.

The Network's first step with the new leader was to evaluate where it was and where it was going. It received a grant from the Gates Foundation to fund a strategic planning project with the Bridgespan Group, Bain Consulting's nonprofit practice.

To evaluate the effectiveness of the schools, the consultants looked beyond the end of high school to college. Although 100 percent of graduates had been accepted into college, only 27 percent were completing college in five years. On one hand, the number was something to celebrate. The college graduation rate was much better than the average for the population Cristo Rey serves. But few were happy with it. School and Network leaders expected more from their program and their graduates.[9] Something had to change.

"We consciously shifted our strategic vision from 'grow, grow, grow' to a focus on quality," Birdsell says. The Bridgespan study had found that the Network was more than a loose association of independent schools, yet it was not a charter management organization.[10] The role of the Network was to lead by influence. To do so, Birdsell and the Network board decided to shut down existing feasibility studies for a year. They looked at both what they could do to help the current schools improve academically and ways to ensure that they would not make the same mistakes again.

Birdsell felt his job was to protect the "brand" of Cristo Rey. The Network and its schools can be compared to a company with franchises. Like Subway, Cristo Rey is the brand, and like the restaurants, its schools are owned and operated locally. A customer at Subway can expect the same quality sandwich in New York as in California and every place between. In the same way, students and their families, donors, work-study sponsors, and colleges should be able to expect students to receive the same quality of education at a Cristo Rey school in Boston or Los Angeles or anywhere in between. "Our board and I believed we had a responsibility, after starting schools, to ensure that the quality given to the students was the best," Birdsell says. "My vision was that we can get better faster together than as singular units."

NEW AND IMPROVED

When the original school in Chicago launched, Preston Kendall remembers that he and his fellow leaders wanted to delay the opening for a year. "There are going to be a ton of problems, whether you open now or if you open in a year, that you're not going to anticipate, so just open it," Kendall says Jesuit provincial Father Brad Schaeffer told the leadership team. "It's not going to be perfect, but just do it."

The "open it now and fix it later" mentality that worked in the booming economy of the 1990s, however, would not continue to work as the economy soured in the late 2000s. Only one school fell victim to the recession, but the lessons the Network learned from it were valuable.

The launch of St. Peter Claver Cristo Rey Catholic High School in Omaha, Nebraska, in 2007 was not unlike those of many other Cristo Rey schools. In the spring before it opened its doors, St. Peter Claver's school leaders were busy fixing up an old elementary school, recruiting faculty and staff, and reviewing the 172 applications.[11] "The Network for the school was developed twelve years ago, but they don't hand you a playbook and say this is what you do. They give you guidelines," Father James Keiter, the school's president, told the *Catholic Voice,* the archdiocesan paper, at the time.

The school, though, had raised less than $2.5 million of its $7 million capital-campaign goal. The start-up principal left the school on short notice just before the school opened. Omaha was also the smallest metropolitan area to have launched a school, which made it more challenging to find corporate work-study jobs. St. Peter Claver opened its doors in the fall, but from the beginning it struggled with admitting and retaining students, finding and keeping corporate job sponsors, and fund-raising. By its fourth year, it only had 205 students and $7 million of debt.[12] On February 11, 2011, the school announced that it would close at the end of the year, its first graduating class being its last.

The Network rethought the feasibility process as a result of Omaha's closing, putting into place a number of safeguards that would prevent future schools from having to close. Instead of waiting for people to come to them and apply to open a Cristo Rey school, Network officials began to proactively seek out markets for schools, targeting cities with more than a million people and preferring states with vouchers or tax-credit programs that can take the burden off of fund-raising. Feasibility-study committees have always been required to interview forty community leaders, one hundred parents, and three hundred young people from low-income families. But the Network learned that schools needed a stronger base of jobs and fund-raising to ensure their success through any economy. Previously, committees only had to have twenty-five letters of intent for jobs signed before the school could be approved, but now they need thirty-five jobs lined up. The cities need to be able to support a school of four to six hundred students, requiring between a hundred and a hundred and fifty full-time equivalent jobs for teams of students, to ensure the financial viability of the school. A school can only grow if the jobs are there to support it.

"I had to say no to a number of communities, but I think we're better off. I think it's better to do it right," Birdsell says. "If you don't have the resources to do this well, don't do it."

The Network board also is stricter with timing and fund-raising. If a prospective school has not raised approximately $2.5 million in gifts and pledges a year before its scheduled opening, it will not open the next year. After starting more than twenty schools, the Network learned that this amount, plus the first year's work-study program and tuition revenue, would cover the launch year and the first year of operation. The Network also requires robust plans and fund-raising prospects to pay for a school building that can accommodate between four and six hundred high-school students.

When Cristo Rey Jesuit College Preparatory School in Houston was being founded, a $1 million gift from Rich and Nancy Kinder boosted the initial fund-raising efforts and allowed the school to open a year earlier than planned. Had the school waited to open until 2010, it is hard to say where the sixty members of the inaugural class of 2013 would be today, board chair Brian Branda points out. Some may not have made it through high school.

The feasibility study also requires schools to put in place a development plan, demonstrating the likelihood that the school will be able to raise funds independently. Through year five, a school will need between $6 and $8 million in donations to cover expenses, the Network estimates.[13] Cristo Rey Houston had planned to raise $10 million by its first graduation, but ended up with $20 million by spring 2013. Because the Kinders are known to be selective in giving to educational institutions, their gift gave Martinez credibility when approaching other donors for major gifts, he says. Martinez's own charisma and unique ability to tell the Cristo Rey story also allowed the school to far exceed its expectation and grow rapidly.

"He's just so engaging that you get sucked into his vortex," says Jeb Bashaw, one of the school's first corporate sponsors. "He's like a little Tasmanian Devil. His enthusiasm brings everyone around him into a great sense of excitement and happiness."

Money is not the only requirement for a successful school launch. School leadership now goes to work a full year before the opening of a new school, rather than just months. Finding the right leaders is key for Cristo Rey schools. "A strong board will hire a strong leader, and a strong leader will hire a strong leadership team," says Jack Crowe, chief operating officer of the Cristo Rey Network, quoting former Network board chair Father Joseph Parkes.

The Houston school's first board chair, Bob Dunn, says that Cristo Rey was like a second job for him during those first few years. "But it's been so much fun, I didn't even pay attention to the time. It's always been a lot more fun than my business," he says. The board was involved in finding the school building, assisting the new staff, and knocking on doors to recruit the first class.

Recruiting students to a school that does not yet exist is the most difficult part of opening a new school. Martinez poured all of his enthusiasm into his uphill admissions sell: "Come to an untested, new educational program; go to school for ten hours a day; work a corporate job as part of your experience; be prepared to have a lot of homework; and be a part of a high school that has no football team—a heresy in the Friday Night Football state of Texas! It is going to be *great*!"

The physical school did not help the sell. True to character, Martinez bought a closed Catholic high school from the archdiocese for $2, twice the ceremonial rate of $1. But he found the abandoned building in disrepair and taken over by vagrants. The school had flooded, and the ceilings were falling in. The front wall had to be held up by scaffolding. Asbestos and mold infected the halls and classrooms. There were broken windows and bullet holes in panes. Even in the school's good days, bars had covered the school's windows. "It looked like you were trapped in a jail," Martinez says. The building was still being renovated into the "corporate, collegiate-like setting" that Martinez envisioned when the school started hosting open houses for prospective students and their families. "Grandmothers are the patron saints of Cristo Rey Jesuit," Martinez says, reflecting back on the early days. "When we were talking to that first class of kids, grandmothers were the first ones to believe."

The admissions process is generous in the first years of a Cristo Rey school, and when schools admit whoever comes to their doors, retention suffers. But as a school gets older, its reputation brings better-qualified applicants. Cristo Rey Jesuit in Houston graduated only sixty in its first class, but today it has far too many applicants for the number of seats available. By its first graduation, the board was already discussing the possibility of opening a second campus on the other side of town.

A System of Accountability

In addition to making changes to the feasibility requirements, the Network created a system of accountability for the schools. Previously, the Network had done collegial visits, "sort of like friends cheering each other on," as Crowe describes it. Now each new school has a Mission Effectiveness Review every year for the first three years, and then all schools have a review every three years after that. The schools are measured on the Mission Effectiveness Standards, which serve as an "early alert system" if something is going wrong.

The Network also publishes the schools' performance on a number of measures, such as retention of students, numbers of alumni going to college, work-study revenue, and fund-raising. Measurement makes it easy to see when a school has a problem.

The Network soon put this system to the test in Brooklyn. Though located in the largest metropolitan area in the country, Cristo Rey Brooklyn High School struggled with finding jobs in the recession. When the school opened in 2008 as Lourdes Academy, the financial crisis was hurting the Wall Street firms and banks that might have been corporate sponsors. But the economy was not the only problem. The school only enrolled forty-three students that first year, fewer than half of the students for a typical Cristo Rey launch and not enough for a sustainable school. "It's really expensive to run a little school," Crowe says.

The Cristo Rey school that those forty-three students walked into might not have been much better than a bad public school. The facility was a small hundred-year-old grade school that had been closed for several years. Even after being fixed up, it was in a state of disrepair, says Christine Román, who came to the school as a math teacher in the fall of 2011. The building did not have a gym, auditorium, science labs, or even a cafeteria kitchen—the school could not provide lunch for its students.

The Network Mission Effectiveness team visited the Brooklyn school in early 2011 to conduct a review of its performance relative to the standards. With 135 students, it was one of the smallest schools in the Network. The school hardly had money for books, Birdsell says, and both school culture and academics suffered without a stable financial base. The metrics warned that the school was in trouble, and the Network advised the school's board of directors that the school was not financially sustainable. The board had recently been reconstituted and was very small, and the report hit its members hard. They came within hours of shutting the school down.

But under the leadership of new board chair Robert Catell, they were unified in their desire to keep the school open. The need for an effective Cristo Rey school in Brooklyn was too great. Catell, a Brooklyn native raised by a single mother, had climbed through the ranks of Brooklyn Union Gas (now National Grid) to become CEO and was key to the company's growth and success. He could relate to Cristo Rey students, even if they were two generations younger, and he and the board were confident that the Brooklyn school could grow with the right leadership and personnel.

After consulting with Parkes, president of the highly successful Cristo Rey New York High School in Harlem, Catell personally recruited Bill Henson to become the school's new president. As a former high-level banking executive, Henson had served on the Harlem school's board and as a full-time director there. Henson also brought on a principal with experience at Cristo Rey New York. The school leaders recruited a whole new faculty and many new key staff members. To take advantage of the national brand, he changed the school's name to Cristo Rey Brooklyn High School.

With more work-study sponsors and donors recruited, the school's finances steadily improved, and enrollment climbed. Román, one of the new teachers at the school, took over as principal for the 2012–13 school year, revamped the discipline program, and started character formation and advisory initiatives. "It seemed like a lot to implement in one year, but it was necessary," she says.

The 2013 graduation—the school's second—gave the school great hope. Though the class of 2013 only had thirty-five students, these students collectively received four hundred college acceptances from one hundred and fifty colleges and $8 million in scholarships and grants.

After graduation, Cristo Rey Brooklyn moved into a new home. It is a typical red brick school, but, unlike the school's previous location, it is a legitimate high-school facility. The new school has an auditorium, a gymnasium, science and computer labs, a cafeteria with a commercial kitchen, a SMARTBoard® in every classroom, and significantly greater instructional space. It is a solid, welcoming space with room to grow. Coupled with the relocation, the school partnered with the nonprofit Boys Hope Girls Hope to manage a boarding program for up to fifty female students. They reside in a former convent on the property from Sunday night through Friday. Cristo Rey Brooklyn is the only school in the Network with a residence program.

A few years after being one meeting away from closing, Cristo Rey Brooklyn is an entirely new place. When Elizabeth Goettl, then head of academics at the Network, came to the school to check up on the academic program in fall 2013, she cried, Román says. "She could not believe how far along we had come in such a short time."

Measurable Metrics for an Ideal

Experience has led the Cristo Rey Network to exact numerical requirements and helpful estimates for jobs and funds required to open a new school. But is that last letter of intent from a corporate work-study sponsor or that final $100,000 donation really going to make a difference in a school's success? Is a student who grows up in a household of four with an annual income of $37,000 that much more "economically disadvantaged" than a student from a family who has $38,000?

"Part of this," Kendall says, "is the whole idea of bringing the ideal to a measurable earthly metric." It is difficult to quantify concepts as "financially sustainable" or "economically disadvantaged," but exact numbers allow for accountability.

When the Gates Foundation asked the Cristo Rey Network for its standards, it also requested data that would allow it to evaluate how well schools were performing against those standards. What started as a thin "statistical directory" has become a 115-page data book published each fall. Today, the Cristo Rey Network data report contains not only test scores, as is to be expected of schools, but also metrics on demographics of the student bodies, school operations, and financial sustainability. Charts document each school's work-study revenue as a percent of the operating budget, its admission funnels of new applicants, and its graduates' persistence in college. There are hopes to expand the use of real-time data across the schools in the future.

It is not enough to collect the data, though; the schools also must use it. School metrics serve the same purpose as classroom evaluations. Cristo Rey teachers are trained in Network professional development sessions to use assessments to see whether their students have learned the material. They may ask students to give a thumbs-up if they understand a concept or they may give them tests. Student feedback and scores are meant to help the teacher decide whether to move on to the next unit or explain the material in a different way.

Likewise, schools can look at the data to see how they can improve their performance. They can look at their peer group of schools—those that opened in the same year—to see how they compare. Many presidents mark up their books, adding questions. The Network can be helpful, Birdsell says, in analyzing the data for larger trends.

Early in Birdsell's Network presidency, his team in the central office noticed an uptick in the average income of students' families. They approached the school administrators at De La Salle North Catholic High School, the Cristo Rey school in Portland, to figure out what was going on there. "They were very open to the criticism," Birdsell says. "If it's grounded in data, nobody can question it."

Since opening in 2001, the school had been recruiting primarily from Catholic middle schools. In the past, they were reliable sources for low-income students, but as Catholic schools became more expensive over the decade, only middle- and upper-class students could be found at those schools. Portland shifted its recruiting strategy to include more charter and public middle schools with low-income students, and its average income metric dropped.

Network staff shared Portland's story with all the schools at the next annual gathering, and the school presidents agreed to make the issue a priority. Simply bringing awareness to the problem helped schools look at what they could do to improve their commitment to serving economically disadvantaged families. School administrators would look at the data book and ask, "Cleveland has kids at $30,000. Why are we at $45,000?" Birdsell says.

Charter schools are often criticized for attracting students who are the cream the crop academically. Cristo Rey Network schools, though, look to serve not the best-performing but the lowest-income students, Crowe says with pride. The average family income for a new class of freshmen has dropped from $37,671 in 2009 to $33,931 in 2013. Although some of the decrease might be due to the state of the economy, much of it is thanks to the schools' holding one another accountable.

RAISING THE BAR IN THE CLASSROOM

Quantifying academic goals may be even more controversial than quantifying financial requirements. Standardized test scores do not reflect students' knowledge and skill, critics complain, especially in low-income and minority communities. By extension, many argue that it is not fair to judge teachers or schools based on test scores.

Indeed, according to test scores, Cristo Rey students should not persist in college at the rates that they are. The ACT test is divided into four subject areas—English, math, reading, and science—each with college-readiness benchmarks. If a student earns a certain score on each test, that student is more likely to do well in corresponding college classes.[14] On average, Cristo Rey students are not yet achieving these college-ready benchmarks. The Cristo Rey class of 2013 had an average ACT composite score of 18.4, compared to a national average of 20.9.

Although test scores alone may have limited value in predicting Cristo Rey students' future success, there must be some measures of growth when the goal is improving students' educational outcomes. Quantifying growth allows the Network to evaluate and tweak its academic program to help students achieve better outcomes. To do so, the Network looks at not simply ACT scores, but also ACT gains, common end-of-the-course exams, the retention of freshmen through graduation, and college enrollment and graduation.

From freshman year through fall of a student's senior year, the Network's interim goal is for students' scores to grow a minimum of 4.5 points on the ACT battery of tests. Ultimately, Goettl says, the ACT growth goal for most Cristo Rey students must be six points for seniors to meet the ACT's college-readiness benchmarks. In the Network's first four-year ACT data set, the class of 2013's average composite score rose 3.2 points from the freshman EXPLORE test to the senior ACT test. (In its growth data, the Network includes only "matched" students, those who have been with them for all four years.) "We've made some progress," Goettl says. "We still have a long way to go, but we're seeing the needle move in the right direction."

The Network also has set goals that 70 percent of students who enroll as freshmen graduate from their Cristo Rey schools, and then that 70 percent of seniors graduate from college within six years. Although four schools already have college graduates, the Cristo Rey Network will evaluate its first significant set of college completion numbers in summer 2014. The class of 2008, which represents ten Cristo Rey schools, will have been out of high school for six years.

The challenge with this metric is that the Cristo Rey class of 2008 experienced a wide variety of academic programs at the ten schools, few of which are used today. At the same time that the class of 2008 was starting college, the Cristo Rey Network was realizing that it could not ask its schools to increase its students' academic outcomes without a plan for how to do so. When the Network turned its attention to student outcomes rather than simply growth, it developed a three-pronged academic initiative to improve the quality of education at Cristo Rey schools. By creating a standards-based curriculum and focusing on teacher effectiveness and instructional leadership, the initiative also put the Cristo Rey Network at the forefront of education reform for more than its work-study program.

From its inception, the Network supported schools with the work-study program, marketing, and development, but individual schools developed their own academic programs, says Goettl. Much of the school-to-school collaboration started with the work-study directors, because their jobs existed nowhere else in education or business. They had to rely on each other. But teachers and principals with expertise in urban education—let alone experience at a school where a quarter of the students leave campus to work every day—are not common either.

Goettl, who had been involved in the Network's Bridgespan

study, looks as though she could belong in the corporate world. She is thin and strong, leading Network meetings in conservative skirt suits. Her background, though, is in education; she was an award-winning principal for years before becoming president of San Miguel High School, the Cristo Rey school in Tucson, Arizona. Goettl talks quickly and confidently about instructional strategies and a standards-based curriculum. Like a walking reference book on education reform, she cites top scholars in the field. She is also organized and precise with her words. After two years at the Network, for instance, she rebranded the Educational Enrichment Initiative as "Teach-Learn-Lead." "An initiative, if you will, comes to an end, but good work around college-ready teaching and learning is too complex to ever come to an end. In high-performing schools, continuous improvement in teaching, learning, and leading never ends," Goettl explains.

Her first priority was the "Learn" portion of "Teach-Learn-Lead"—creating a standards-based curriculum or, as she calls it, the *what* of education. She invited all the schools to participate in the initial curriculum development in the spring of 2009, and eight schools sent their principal and a team of teachers. Using research and state and national standards, they made decisions on what Cristo Rey students should know and be able to do at the end of their four years of high school in all core subjects. Then they planned backward. Rather than starting where students are and taking them as far in their knowledge and abilities as time allows, they looked at what every student needs to know and be able to do to be college ready. If students must demonstrate certain math knowledge and skills by senior year, what do they need to learn as juniors, sophomores, and freshmen?

Seven schools field-tested the curriculum that fall and were able to provide feedback when the group gathered again the next summer. By then, the Common Core State Standards had been released. So the team aligned the Cristo Rey curriculum with the new math and English language arts standards.

More Cristo Rey schools have adopted the curriculum every year since then. A few schools, having already gone through their own curriculum development process, chose to retain their current programs. All new schools receive support to implement the common Cristo Rey curriculum. By 2014, twenty-five out of twenty-eight schools had adopted it.

Coming together to create a curriculum allowed schools to pool their collective knowledge, employing economies of scale to solve a common problem. The ready-made curriculum was a huge help when launching Cristo Rey Philadelphia High School, says Michael Gomez, principal of one of the youngest Cristo Rey schools. There are enough questions to deal with when launching a new school. Being able to give teachers a framework that they can work within allows the school to focus on other questions.

Patricia Weitzel-O'Neill, the Boston College education professor who was superintendent of Catholic schools in Washington, DC, sees that schools with a collaborative network are the ones doing the best work for their students. "That's a richness. The Network provides the leadership in these individual schools with access to resources that they would otherwise not have," she says. "The stand-alone school all by itself is not going to make it."

Goettl and Weitzel-O'Neill emphasize that standards do not tell Cristo Rey teachers how to teach. A common Network curriculum seems counter to the individualized learning that characterized the original Cristo Rey school, but it is not.

"There's a lack of understanding right now about curriculum and curriculum standards," Weitzel-O'Neill says. "Common Core Standards are amazing, because they're skill based. They don't say what you teach; they say what a student needs to be able to *do* with literature, the kinds of books students need to know how to read, digest, critically evaluate, and analyze, and then move forward to the next level of thinking. That's much, much more difficult for teachers."

Teacher effectiveness is a critical component for successful schools. To help teachers figure out how best to teach these new standards, the Network also began offering professional development for teachers, the "Teach" of "Teach-Learn-Lead." "Once you've gotten clear about the *what*, then you focus on the *how*," Goettl says.

The Network brings a number of teachers to Chicago each summer for professional development; 225, nearly half of all Cristo Rey teachers nationwide, participated in the 2013 sessions. Sixty new teachers were trained in the common curriculum, learning how to plan lessons starting at the goal and working backward, just as the curriculum itself was created. All teachers learn high-impact instructional strategies—teaching methods proven to be effective in high-performing classrooms across the United States. The use of learning goals or objectives for lessons, for instance, is common across Cristo Rey classrooms—and all good classrooms, Goettl adds. Professional development sessions also support work introduced by the Common Core State Standards, such as disciplinary literacy. Students need to be able to read and write technical text, for instance, so the sessions train science teachers in instructional shifts that allow them to help students comprehend complex science articles, analyze data, or use text evidence to support their responses.

The Summer Institute also gives teachers another resource for help during the year: each other. John Stradley, the English teacher at Verbum Dei in Los Angeles, was involved in the development of the Network curriculum and then participated in Network professional development. He bounces lesson ideas off both his colleagues in the school and English teachers in New York, he says. Along with a teacher from San Miguel in Tucson, he also shared with principals and presidents at a national conference how his "double-dose" writing class helps catch freshmen up on basic skills. "I'm never one to turn down a trip across the country," Stradley laughs. "But I was actually pleased to talk about what we're doing here, because I'm proud of our achievements. I left that meeting feeling that I was part of something that was bigger than Verbum Dei High School," he adds.

A significant portion of teachers attend professional development, but not all can, and those sessions may be far from teachers' minds by the next February. Professional development, therefore, must continue at the schools. To encourage a culture of continuous growth within the schools, the third piece of the Network's academic program, "Lead," helps principals be leaders of learning rather than the manager-leaders of yesterday's Catholic schools. Principals have their own professional development sessions and access to Network-sponsored leadership coaching. They meet in person throughout the year—at a principals' meeting in January, the national conference in the spring, Summer Institute sessions, and in leadership coaching cohorts.

As the newest principal in the room at the 2013 conference, Christine Román, of Cristo Rey Brooklyn, says she could not have taken on the job of principal without the support of the Network resources and the help of her fellow principals. Román started her career in Texas, teaching for five years and taking on some leadership roles there. But then she left teaching to look for a greater challenge; she had felt a need to do something "more prestigious" than teaching. Román earned a master's degree in public health from Columbia University and then worked at the university doing research and data analysis. "But deep in my heart, I'm an educator. It is what I believe my vocation is and what God sent me into this world to do," she says.

Román found Cristo Rey Brooklyn and restarted her teaching career, soon impressing Bill Henson, the new president, who was working to turn the struggling school around. She interviewed to become an assistant principal, a position that would provide her with more of a challenge, and was offered the job. But when the principal gave birth to her first child and eventually decided to stay home, Román stepped into the principal role during her first year at the school.

Under Henson's leadership, the Brooklyn school had begun to improve from its rocky beginnings. It had a new faculty, more work-study sponsors, better fund-raising, and plans to move into a new building. Still, when she moved from teacher to principal,

Román felt alone as a "rookie," she told her fellow principals at the annual conference. She had little experience or training in school leadership. Then she went to the annual principals' meeting in January and realized others were doing the exact work that she had undertaken. Moreover, it was the type of environment where it was acceptable to say, "I don't know."

After that meeting, she started scheduling visits to schools in her region, so that she could see how other Cristo Rey principals led their schools. "Everyone was so willing and open to welcome me to their school and have me there, teach me, mentor me, show me what they were doing, and be honest about what was working and not working," Román says.

At the end of one session at the 2013 conference, Román expressed her thanks and called on her fellow principals to take advantage of resources that they could provide each other. In an impassioned speech, she encouraged her colleagues not to wait for meetings or annual conferences to reach out to each other. "We are one Cristo Rey school," Román told her colleagues.

"If we were able to turn this school around, we owe it to the mentorship and the coaching from other principals and coaches," Román says. "You cannot do these things all alone. That's the beauty of being part of a network."

A COLLABORATIVE FUTURE

At its core, the role of the Network is to facilitate such collaboration. Professionals at all levels make connections across the Network. In addition to the national conference, school leaders work together regularly. Presidents have started taking an annual retreat together. Principals and work-study directors both have separate annual meetings. Teachers primarily meet through professional development meetings in Chicago, and the academic personnel are active on SharePoint, a web-based communication tool through which they can access resources and engage in discussions.

Teachers are not the only ones to receive professional development. There are cohort groups for nearly every position at the schools—CFOs, development directors, admissions directors, and college counselors, for instance—and all have regularly met in Chicago. The Network has started regional conferences for work-study coordinators, the junior staff in the office, as well.

Although work-study directors have always compared notes on how to run their programs, the Network office also encourages ongoing collaboration through cross-selling their accounts with other schools. The Network maintains a database of companies that the schools work with, and many of the companies are national. If a potential corporate sponsor in Atlanta has an office in Houston, the Houston school might be able to make the right introductions for the Atlanta school.

But spreading that information through a database is insufficient, work-study directors say. Cross-selling takes personal relationships, and conferences allow colleagues in the same field to get to know each other better. Good experiences can spread across cities, but so too can bad experiences, some worry. Before they risk a loyal corporate sponsor, they need to be able to trust their colleagues across the country and their programs.

The Network also helps work-study directors figure out how to train their students for work. Despite having access to a pool of talented teachers within their school, teachers and the work-study staff rarely have the time to bring lessons of education into the work program and vice versa. Through surveying corporate sponsors and seeing what skills students do and do not have, work-study directors have determined that they need to teach computer skills and communication skills to give students the ability to adapt in the changing job market. But they have struggled with how to teach those skills. PowerPoint presentations that work in corporate meetings do not often fly with high-school students.

Ken Malik, the national work-study director at the Cristo Rey Network, is shaping a work-study curriculum for the summer training program. As he puts it, he is "plagiarizing" the best practices from multiple schools. "Just like you would with a product, you build it, you test it, and then you make modifications based on that," he explains. Rather than having to reinvent the wheel, new schools will eventually be given a package on how to run a work-study training program, just as they have a curriculum for their academic program. Existing schools will not be forced to implement the new curriculum, but Malik hopes the Network will be able to influence them by demonstrating results.

At the national conference, work-study directors present to each other their best practices for training and new industries that they are targeting for jobs. "We have to rely on our lieutenants on the ground, who are our corporate work-study directors, for what's going to work for them," Malik says.

From Kendall's perspective as a school leader, a military analogy also captures the relationship between schools and the Network. "We're down here in the trenches fighting the good fight, and we need some generals up on the hill making sure we don't get outflanked," he says. As the generals, the Network can stay on top of trends in education and the workplace—such as the importance of cognitive skills or jobs of the future.

At the same time, the generals on the hill give the lieutenants the freedom to exercise creativity. A perennial conversation in the Network is how much room there is for freedom within the Cristo Rey model of education. "Are you trying to stamp out identical replications, or is this a model that we can tweak and massage to our personal, local needs?" as Kendall phrases the question.

The sharing of ideas and experimentation with how to apply them is a good reason that not all schools should be the same. The constant striving to do things better, after all, is what keeps the schools on the cutting edge of education reform. "We don't want to stifle new ideas," Kendall says. But at the same time, the Mission Effectiveness Standards keep Cristo Rey schools true to their core values.

Cristo Rey Central

The push to keep the Cristo Rey Network schools at the front of education reform requires a strong central office. Although two people work directly on the feasibility studies, all lend their expertise and assistance with the opening of new schools. Network staffers are often on the road to visit schools, provide assistance, and ensure that they are following the Mission Effectiveness Standards.

As experts in their fields, the Network staff can help schools implement the best practices, recognize the good ideas of one school, and make sure they are spread to other schools. In addition to Malik and Goettl, who work on the work-study and academic programs, the Network has added two staff members to focus on helping Cristo Rey graduates succeed in college, the ninth Mission Effectiveness Standard. The Network has developed alliances with more than forty University Partners around the country to support Cristo Rey graduates. Those schools give Cristo Rey students a holistic review of their applications and provide support to students who enroll. The Network also organizes annual conferences for the University Partners, so that they too can share best practices for serving low-income college students.

Not all Cristo Rey students, however, go to these forty partner schools, so the Network has started reaching out to alumni in person and online and supporting schools' efforts to connect with their alumni. In a pilot program supported by the Michael and Susan Dell Foundation, three schools are testing out an alumni tracking system that will help the schools ensure that their graduates are on the path to college graduation.

These new initiatives and the push to improve Cristo Rey schools' outcomes have required some growth in the Network staff. As at any major nonprofit, there are programmatic staffers, along with communications, business, and administrative personnel.

Education organizations face a common concern when expanding. The track records of public-school districts make some educators weary of the centralization of control. Catholic educators in particular value subsidiarity, the idea of making decisions on the most local level possible. The local nature of Catholic schools is often credited with their success, because teachers and principals are able to meet the needs of their students rather than seek approval for some initiative from a central office. The intent of public-school bureaucracies was to offer equal educational opportunities, but the requests and demands from the district can become burdensome.

When the first Cristo Rey school started, in contrast, the founders wanted to keep its size reasonable, not only for the students but also for the adults, Preston Kendall says. "At some point, you cannot get the entire faculty and staff in one room and make a decision."

Even with more feasibility studies in the works, the central office will not grow substantially beyond its current fourteen employees, says Crowe, the Network's COO. At its current staff level, the Network will be able to continue to lead by example, but it does not have the capacity to centralize decision making.

The Network will open approximately two schools a year in target markets, toward the goal of having forty schools open by 2020. Half the growth of the Network, though, will come from existing schools. Based on modeling of current growth, the Cristo Rey Network will have fifteen thousand students and twenty-two thousand Cristo Rey alumni by 2020, maintaining its position as the largest organization of independent high schools serving low-income youth. By 2020, five thousand of those graduates will have already finished college, making the Cristo Rey Network a leader in developing low-income college graduates as well. To achieve these numbers, the Network will continue to work with its schools on refining its program, with technology in the classroom, better metrics for student success, a stronger work-study curriculum, and support for alumni, to name a few ongoing initiatives.

The vision for the Cristo Rey Network is "growth and quality," Crowe says. "We're at a point now where it's not okay to do one or the other. We can grow the mission, and we're mission driven. We need to support our schools and grow in a reasonable fashion."

Part II

Students Who Work

CHAPTER FOUR

Lifelong Learners

There's an assumption that "Catholics know how to do schools," says Elizabeth Goettl, the former chief academic officer of the Cristo Rey Network. But when it comes to inner-city schools serving low-income families, she suggests, the early Cristo Rey academic results indicated that most students were making limited academic gains. Catholic schools may provide advantages over some inner-city public schools—a caring but disciplined environment and a safe place for learning—but students need strong academic preparation to succeed in college and beyond.

When the original Cristo Rey Jesuit High School started in 1996, principal Sister Judy Murphy, OSB, saw an opportunity not just to fund Catholic education, but also to make it work better for low-income families. She asked teachers to look at their student body and personalize the education for those students. Teachers would work together to try to figure out the best way to teach the students to become lifelong learners.

Early on, history teacher Mike Heidkamp developed a civics class for seniors designed to help them become independent scholars before college. After a unit on psychology, though, a student handed him a two-page letter explaining that she felt she needed to learn historical events and dates before college. When Heidkamp polled the class, the students agreed.[1] So he veered from his syllabus and assigned them a new project: the students were to find out what they needed to learn to be prepared for college. They interviewed other teachers and sent e-mails to college professors. The professors, the students found out, agreed with Heidkamp. Rather than list wars or historical events that they should know about, the professors said students needed to learn how to think critically, write well, and speak well.[2]

Little did Heidkamp or his students know then that their informal study replicated, albeit on a much smaller scale, a prominent education researcher's methods. David Conley, a University of Oregon professor and founder of the Educational Policy Improvement Center, is an expert in college readiness. In his research, Conley has surveyed university faculty members multiple times to find out what is required for success in their entry-level courses. In his first study, more than four hundred professors almost unanimously agreed that, in addition to knowing content, "students needed to know what to do with the content they were learning."[3]

In the years since Heidkamp's experimental class, the Cristo

Rey academic program has evolved. Learning from experience and research on what works to educate students from low-income communities, the Cristo Rey Network has developed a core college-preparatory curriculum and professional development program to support teachers in increasing student achievement. But the idea behind the Network academic program remains true to the ethos of the original school in its early years. The Network understands where its students start—often multiple years behind—but sets its expectations high: college readiness. To get there requires teaching students to become lifelong learners.

A National Shift in Education Policy

Although it is not a given that a Catholic school will have a superior academic program, research from the 1980s and early 1990s indicates that, even when controlled for other variables, Catholic schools serve low-income students better than public schools. Studies at the time hoped to glean lessons from what Catholics were doing right for use in public schools.[4] An essential piece of the Catholic school equation, they determined, was that these schools taught everyone a college-prep curriculum. Cristo Rey's academic program is best understood within the national shift in education policies toward preparing every student for college.

In the 1980s, public-school educators started rethinking the "comprehensive" education model, which tracked students who were not "college material" into vocational or general studies. The shift to a knowledge-based economy meant that high-school students could no longer take their skills from shop class and find a stable, good-paying job at a factory. Educators were beginning to see that some people—often those from low-income communities—were simply left behind in the new economy.

States' first effort to correct this problem was to increase the number of classes required for graduation. The average number of credits increased from 17.3 to 19.8 from 1980 to 1993.[5] But more did not necessarily mean better. Next, states started to specify what classes a student should take to earn a high-school degree, not allowing remedial classes, such as "business math," to pass for academic courses. Still, not all Algebra I classes are created equal. Classes with the same name might be taught differently across the hall from each other, let alone across the state.

In an effort to make sure that Victor in Watts would be taught the same thing as Bobby in Beverly Hills, educators turned toward standards—a uniform set of knowledge and skills that students should have at a certain level of schooling, no matter where their classroom is. In 2001, President George W. Bush's landmark educational legislation, "No Child Left Behind," mandated that states adopt standards-based education. Students also had to be tested to make sure that they were meeting the standards, with consequences for schools that did not prepare students adequately. The bill passed with bipartisan support. The ideas that all students deserve an equal education and that schools should be held accountable are still widely accepted, though implementation of these ideas remains problematic.

Educational researcher David Conley writes, "Standards were

little more than codifications of basic skills and current content taught at each grade level."[6] Even as it became clear that some postsecondary education was necessary for employment in today's economy, state standards only promoted the goal of high-school completion. Moreover, the standards and the levels required for "proficiency" varied from state to state, resulting in great inequalities. "Sometimes too much variation can be a bad thing," Conley writes.[7]

The Common Core State Standards—along with the Next Generation Science Standards—were a response to these problems. With the support of foundations like the Bill and Melinda Gates Foundation, the national associations for governors and school officers came together to bring equality and greater rigor to state standards with the Common Core. Forty-five states have voluntarily adopted the new standards, many aiming for full implementation in 2014.

The Common Core sets standards that define college readiness in English language arts and math. Planning backward from college readiness, it then sets standards for each grade level that build to the final goal. In the writing standards, for instance, drawing a picture in kindergarten becomes writing to convey ideas and information by third grade, which becomes conveying complex ideas accurately "through the effective selection, organization, and analysis of content" by high-school graduation.[8] The English language arts standards emphasize literacy across disciplines, research and critical thinking, and the ability to craft and communicate arguments clearly through both writing and speaking. The math standards and the Next Generation Science Standards both emphasize not only facts to be learned, but also "practices," such as modeling and abstract and quantitative reasoning, that help students understand what they are doing.

The new trend in these national standards is "fewer, clearer, and higher." The level of content knowledge required for college readiness, Conley explains, "is nowhere near what people think it is. You need a specific, greater area of expertise based on your area of interest in college, but to get into college, the foundational skills are relatively modest, and a lot of them are introduced in middle school."[9] Still, many worry about the level of rigor. In New York, less than a third of students passed Common Core–aligned tests in 2013, and many teachers complained that they had not been prepared well enough to implement the new standards.[10]

The critics of the Common Core are correct that it "is not a panacea for America's education woes."[11] Chicago Public Schools have implemented a "college prep for all" curriculum since 1997, and yet student outcomes have not substantially improved.[12] A college-prep curriculum will not be successful, researchers looking at Chicago have concluded, "without attending to many other issues plaguing high schools, such as unmotivated and unprepared students, lackluster instruction, or teachers unprepared to instruct heterogeneous classes."[13]

Conley puts it bluntly: "Common Core is going in the right direction, but it's a recipe for disaster if we don't address the broader questions and issues. We're not teaching kids how to manage the learning process, and we're not teaching them how to think."[14]

Schools need to engage students in their learning, making it relevant to their lives, and focus on learning skills and techniques as well as cognitive strategies.

WHAT IS COLLEGE READINESS?

A year before the Common Core State Standards were released, Goettl gathered a team of principals and teachers from Cristo Rey schools to develop the Cristo Rey Network curriculum—a set of standards that all member schools could use to get their students ready for college. As many states did in the 1990s, the team outlined what classes every Cristo Rey student is required to take before graduation:

- Four years of college-ready math
- Four years of English language arts
- Four years of science
- Three years of social studies
- Three years of world language
- Four years of theology

States have increased the number of classes required for high-school graduation in the last thirty years, but few require quite as many classes as the Cristo Rey curriculum. When you add in other state requirements that apply to Cristo Rey schools, such as physical education, the schedule leaves little room for electives. Within this rigorous lineup of classes, Cristo Rey Network standards incorporate into all classes both the content and the critical-thinking skills that Cristo Rey graduates will need for college.

Like the creators of the newest generation of standards, the Cristo Rey team started with their end goal: college readiness. With only 27 percent of Cristo Rey alumni graduating from college, they knew they could prepare students better. They brought in David Conley and looked at other models of college readiness to understand what their students would need to know and be able to do to be successful in college.

Cristo Rey schools' struggle to prepare students for college is a common issue. Since the mid-1970s, the percentage of U.S. high-school graduates who immediately enroll in a community college or four-year institution has risen to 68 percent, Conley reports, yet 40 percent or more of these students must take remedial courses.[15] In other words, less than 30 percent of high-school graduates are ready to succeed in college straight out of high school.

A significant portion of Conley's work in education has been to figure out how to make the transition between high school and college smoother. To do so, he has developed a four-part model of college readiness for high schools:

- **Think**—*Key Cognitive Skills:* formulating a problem, researching, interpreting information
- **Know**—*Key Content Knowledge:* learning technical knowledge and skills in English, math, and other subjects; understanding what it takes to learn

- **Act**—*Key Learning Skills and Techniques:* learning skills like goal setting and self-awareness; learning techniques like time management and study skills
- **Go**—*Key Transition Knowledge and Skills:* understanding college admissions, choosing a career path, and learning to be a self-advocate

Key Cognitive Skills are the critical-thinking skills that the first teachers of Cristo Rey knew were so important. In college, students must be able to formulate a problem, do research, interpret information, and communicate with precision and accuracy.

At the same time, Heidkamp's students in his civics class were right in that there was certain Key Content Knowledge that they needed to know before making it to college. The level of technical knowledge and skills that a student must master depends on the student's major. Cristo Rey schools, though, want to give their students the option to pursue any career path they choose. Students cannot pursue STEM (science, technology, engineering, and math) majors if they are missing key content knowledge from their high-school science program.

Key Learning Skills and Techniques are the methods students use to take ownership of their learning—setting goals, monitoring their own progress, and seeking help—as well as practices such as time management, strategic reading, and test-taking skills.

Key Transition Knowledge and Skills covers college counseling. Because Cristo Rey students are often the first ones in their family to go to college, they rely on the school to teach them what they need to know about college. Many students come in not knowing that GPA stands for grade point average, let alone how it is calculated or why it is important. Students and parents need to be taught the term FAFSA—and how to fill out the financial-aid forms. They also need to be familiarized with the culture of college campuses and understand how to advocate for oneself and pursue a major and a career. In its ongoing effort to help its students succeed in college, the Network has developed a college-counseling curriculum. Most schools have a weekly college counseling class that all students take from second semester of their junior year through fall semester of their senior year.

There are other models of college readiness as well. In developing its academic plan, the Cristo Rey team also looked at the framework from the Partnership for 21st Century Skills, a coalition of the business, community, and education leaders and policy makers. Its model of student outcomes includes core subjects, life and career skills, learning and innovation skills, and information, media, and technology skills.

The Common Core State Standards offer another definition of college readiness within subject areas. Some schools are in states that require private schools to align with the Common Core. Because the Cristo Rey curriculum is based on the same research, it was not difficult to align the Cristo Rey standards with the Common Core State Standards.

High-performing schools focus on continuous improvement, Goettl says. Goettl received unanimous support from principals implementing the program to refine the initial standards for English language arts, math, and science in 2013. The revised standards organize the curriculum benchmarks into three levels of complexity, allowing teachers to better organize their instruction, so that it grows in complexity throughout the year and over the four years of high school. The Cristo Rey curriculum is now closely aligned with both the Common Core State Standards and ACT's College and Career Readiness Standards. The ACT test is not an arbitrary measure of college readiness, but rather is based on standards of what students need to know and do for success in college.

Various theories of college readiness can be seen played out in Cristo Rey classrooms. Though each group may describe what students need to know and be able to do differently, they all come down to a similar ethos, Conley says. The new approaches "emphasize the role of the learner as a processor of information and creator of meaning," he writes in a book explaining the shift in standards to educators. "For learning to be deeper, it must be active, engaging, social, self-monitored, and self-aware."[16]

MIDDLE-SCHOOL SKILLS

While policy makers and academics strive to ensure that no children are left behind, Cristo Rey's challenge is educating students who have already been left behind. The schools have come up with a variety of ways—doubling class times for English and math, offering summer or after-school enrichment, and connecting students with tutors—to help freshmen catch up and build a strong foundation for a college-preparatory education.

During a peer-tutoring session at Cristo Rey Boston, freshman Serge Beauvais is getting help from his friend Devon Arias in math. Devon asks Serge to figure out how many minutes there are in four days. "Before you start, talk through it, so you don't rush," advises Doug McNicol, the full-time volunteer running Boston's proficiency program for freshmen. All freshmen at Cristo Rey Boston must pass a grammar and math test at 90 percent to ensure they have mastered their middle-school skills.

Writing out his steps on the whiteboard, Serge correctly figures out that there are 1,440 minutes in a day, but then he makes a mistake on the second step. Devon chides him in a way only a peer can and corrects his mistake. They move on to basic geometry. This time, Serge is stumped. He has to ask Devon for the formula for the area of the circle.

It took Devon multiple times to pass the math proficiency test. Silly mistakes often hold students back from passing, but Devon knows the material. The act of taking a test over and over again teaches testing-taking skills—an essential learning skill—as well as concentration and perseverance. Some students pass on their own, or McNicol may organize a review session for a group of students to brush up on a few types of questions. For students like Serge, though, more intensive tutoring—from a teacher, volunteer, or fellow student—is important. By analyzing test scores, McNicol can identify the types of questions that a student needs to work on, such as word problems or geometry, so that tutoring sessions are used efficiently.

By the end of the school year, Serge passed his math test. McNicol sits down with the students individually after they pass and shows them a graph of their scores throughout the year. They can see the upward trend and understand that, with effort, they can learn and improve—a lesson as essential as the area of a circle for budding lifelong learners. Students complain that it is a frustrating and annoying process, but they also say that passing the test gives them a sense of achievement. It is a rite of passage, McNicol says.

Intervention strategies for freshmen are as much about key learning techniques and skills as they are about the key content knowledge. At Christ the King Preparatory School, the Cristo Rey school in Newark, New Jersey, students complain about Cornell notes as much as Boston's freshmen complain about the proficiency program. As freshmen, all students are required to use this note-taking strategy in class, dividing their paper into three sections, one for key points and terms, one for notes, and one for a summary.

Cornell notes are a waste of paper, a group of sophomores agree, but they unanimously and enthusiastically say that yes, of course, they still take notes, another critical learning skill. They laugh and compare how many notebooks each goes through in a year. "Trees are *used* in this school," Emilia Glass says. Though she is now a good student, she calls her freshman year her "worst year in school history" due to the transition from eighth grade to a college-prep high school. "It was way more work than I was used to," she says. "When I was in middle school, I never took notes. Here, I know if I don't write this down, I'm not going to remember."

"And you have to understand what you learn as opposed to remembering it," another sophomore girl adds.

Christ the King freshmen also are required to stay after school three days a week for Homework Center. Students earn their way out of the after-school program by maintaining at least a 77 percent in all of their classes. After first-quarter grades come out, older students who are failing a class also are assigned to Homework Center. "It's really a proactive approach to instilling good study habits and underlining the importance of homework completion," says Pamela Rauscher, Christ the King's dean of academics.

As some students get ready to go home—talking, laughing, and slamming their lockers shut—others settle in for their "tenth period" of work. Some sit quietly and use the time to finish their homework before heading home. In a computer lab, students log on to Study Island, an Internet-based learning tool that allows students to go through practice problems. They can also use the time to work with teachers. Some days, a volunteer will come in—with donuts—and lead a discussion of what the freshmen are learning in history. When the volunteer compares the printing press to the proliferation of cell phones during one session, the students are incredulous. Nonetheless, his relaxed way of covering the material seems to work, Rauscher says.

"We do have students who start out failing and at some point turn it around," Rauscher says. Her list of students assigned to Homework Center is filled with freshmen and sophomores, but by junior year the number of students on academic probation drops dramatically, while the number of those on the honor roll rises.

Across the Network, the number of students involved in an academic intervention mirror those in Newark's Homework Center. Freshmen are typically involved in more than one intervention program, but by the time they are seniors, few need the extra assistance, and when they do, they are more able to seek it out themselves.

Each day, about half a dozen students come to Homework Center who are not required to do so. Sophomore Joseph Dillard does so because it is easier than working at home. He has to take two bus rides to get home after school. When he gets home, he showers and eats, then helps younger siblings. "That's too much, and we're human," he says. At the Homework Center he can focus and get his work done. When he is finished with all of his responsibilities at home, then he will review his notes and study. "The teachers are here to help us, but it's up to the student to take initiative," Joseph says. "When you get through it and you get that A or that B, you feel accomplished, and you say, 'If I can do it here, I can do it anywhere.'"

Academic interventions are about teaching students how academia works, says John Stradley, the English teacher who was one of the first in the Network to teach a "double dose" of freshman English at Verbum Dei High School in Los Angeles. In addition to teaching prepositions and vocabulary in his writing course, he teaches freshmen the process of writing a research paper, from finding and analyzing sources and creating note cards to structuring paragraphs and using proper citations. The freshman-year paper allows other teachers to assign more complex research papers in higher-level courses, knowing that all students have already gone through the process at least once. For many freshmen, it is the first time they will have written a paper in the formal style required by college professors.

As a freshman in Stradley's first-period writing class, Miguel Rios answers questions about prepositions correctly. Still, he is not a perfect student, often struggling with comprehension, Stradley and his other teachers say. When Stradley assigned the research paper, though, Miguel surprised him. "Thank you for challenging us," Miguel said to his teacher.

A Classroom with an Agenda

When students walk into Christina D'Emma's English class at Cristo Rey Philadelphia High School, they know the routine. D'Emma has projected her computer screen on the whiteboard. "Do Now," a PowerPoint slide says, with a few lines of text lacking punctuation or capitalizations. "I'm starting the timer right now," D'Emma says when the bell rings, and students turn to a worksheet with the same lines of text to correct them. As the students finish, they rise to their feet, and D'Emma circulates the room checking papers.

All their classes at Cristo Rey Philadelphia begin with a "do now" exercise and prayer. They also include a "total engagement strategy" that involves all students and a "summarizer," a few questions that allow students to process the lesson and teachers to check for understanding. Every minute is planned with intention in a Cristo Rey classroom. Class time is valuable, since students are only in class four days a week, but it is also a best practice for teachers to have a well-planned agenda. Many of the strategies Cristo Rey teachers employ in their classrooms are not unusual, Goettl says. They are simply good teaching.

A few of D'Emma's students do not finish correcting the sentence in one minute, but they can complete it as homework, she says. D'Emma advances the PowerPoint to a prayer from St. Francis de Sales. The students promise to accept difficulties and conduct themselves during this day in a manner pleasing to God—a prayer that seems to be written for a Catholic college-prep high school in an inner-city neighborhood.

D'Emma flips to the next slide with the homework assignment for the coming night, making sure that all students write it down in their planners. She advances the PowerPoint to the learning goal: "As a college-bound student, I can define and identify figurative language in 'The Scarlet Ibis.'" James Hurst's short story about two brothers is used to introduce freshmen to symbolism. D'Emma has a student read it aloud, while the rest of the students write it down in their notes. A learning goal or objective for the day can be found posted in most classrooms across the Cristo Rey Network. Teachers want their students to understand not only the lesson, but also why the lesson is important and how it fits into their education.

D'Emma also wants her students to see their homework as a productive tool to help them learn. One of the most effective ways to encourage students to complete their homework, teachers agree, is to make it relevant to the class discussion. D'Emma uses a common instructional strategy called "think, pair, share" to review the previous night's homework. Students have already thought about various symbols used in literature at home; then they pair up to discuss their findings with a classmate; and finally

D'Emma cold-calls a few people to share with the entire class. The vast majority of students are ready with not only a symbol, but also what it means. One girl, though, admits that she did not do her homework. D'Emma asks her partner, and he answers in one word: "Lion."

"And what did you learn about lion?" D'Emma says, pushing him farther.

"It's a very diverse symbol."

"What could it represent?" D'Emma asks again, not letting him opt out of the question.

"Strength," he responds quietly.

"Good," D'Emma says, moving on to another student.

The instructional strategies that teachers in Cristo Rey schools use are designed to help students take ownership of their learning. Although these strategies are not unique to Cristo Rey classrooms, the Cristo Rey Network teacher training allows schools to implement them effectively across all classrooms.

Traditionally, some high-school teachers have used "spray and pray lecturing," as Goettl says. "I'm going to spit it out and hope you catch it." Educators describe the shift in a teacher's role as moving from "the sage on the stage" to "a guide on the side." As a guide, teachers emphasize student engagement and application of learning. They call on students out of the blue and spend as much time in the back of the classroom or circulating around the room as they do in front of the whiteboard.

A math teacher at Cristo Rey Boston, for instance, tries to engage more students in lessons by choosing one student to write answers on the board and another to call on classmates. When she asks a question, she also asks whether the class agrees with the answer. If some disagree, she will ask them to explain why, but even when the whole class agrees on the right answer, she has her student helper call on somebody to explain the correct answer. She also has enough time to check in with a struggling student sitting in the back row with his head down.

One of D'Emma's colleagues at Cristo Rey Philadelphia employs the same agree/disagree strategy, but she has a jar of Popsicle sticks, each with a student's name on it. As she asks a question, she pulls out a stick and cold-calls on the student.

Student engagement is what Cristo Rey Philadelphia principal Michael Gomez looks for when he observes classrooms. He looks not only at what the teacher is doing, but also at what the students are doing. "Is every student thinking at every desk, and what's the data to prove it?" he says. In addition to test scores, classroom observations allow him to collect "evidence." All students in a classroom should be able to tell him what they are learning in that class period.

The learning goal offers teachers a framework for evaluating their work. The evaluation process becomes less subjective when centered on the learning goal and whether it was accomplished. It depersonalizes the process of classroom observation, Gomez says. "All you're talking about is evidence: What happened here, why did it happen, and how did it happen?"

Ideally, the learning goal is not just about content, but also higher-order thinking skills. By the end of D'Emma's class, she will have students not only identifying metaphors, similes, and allusions in a text, but also writing their own. Her summarizing activity asks students to fill in the blanks to describe a character in

"The Scarlet Ibis": "If brother were a season he would be _____, because . . ."

Digging Deeper

The lesson on *defining* and *identifying* figurative language was part of a larger fiction unit. After reading "The Scarlet Ibis," D'Emma assigned her students an essay asking them to "*analyze the figurative language, imagery, and symbolism James Hurst employs to develop the theme of excessive pride in the story.*"

Teachers must be very precise about the words they use, Gomez says. They look at the action verbs from Bloom's taxonomy, a classification of learning objectives, when writing their learning goals. The verbs fall into six categories of increasing levels of learning. After building knowledge, students must understand, apply, analyze, evaluate, and finally create.

Verbs like *define* and *identify* fall under the knowledge level— completely appropriate for an introduction to figurative language, Gomez says. More advanced learning goals might include words like *explain* or *distinguish* (understand), *illustrate* or *interpret* (apply), *compare* or *classify* (analyze), *criticize* or *defend* (evaluate), and finally *anticipate* or *design* (create). Students may not remember the figurative language in "The Scarlet Ibis" by the time they reach college, but they will have gained the ability to understand, use, and create such language.

At Cristo Rey schools, education is about more than facts learned. It is also about "the skill of transfer," Gomez says.

"They're learning a skill and then they're using it in a different way. That's how we think students are going to remember and actually learn the skill or information. They're not learning just to memorize it; they're learning so that they can use it in a different situation."

To encourage deeper learning—in which students become processors and creators of knowledge rather than just recipients of it—Cristo Rey teachers are intentional about incorporating attitudes, behaviors, and thinking strategies into their classroom lessons.

At Cristo Rey Jesuit College Preparatory School in Houston, every classroom has a picture of a brain lifting weights at the front of the classroom. Principal Katherine Cater points to the illustration in her office. It is all over the school, she explains, to remind students to have a "growth mind-set." Stanford psychologist Carol Dweck has shown that people with a growth mind-set—who view intelligence as malleable—do much better academically than those with a "fixed mind-set," who see intelligence as unchanging. Students, moreover, can be taught to have a growth mind-set.[17]

When students are struggling with a problem, a teacher can point to the brain lifting weights to remind them of their ability to learn. Students also remind each other that their brains can grow, Cater says.

Although many in the education world agree that attitudes, behaviors, and thinking skills are important to academic achievement, there is no one uniform way to talk about them. The Common Core math standards and the Next Generation Science Standards list eight "practices." Students, for example, must "make sense of problems and persevere in solving them."[18] Some refer to such skills alternately as "cognitive," "noncognitive," or "metacognitive."

When Cater went to a Network session on cognitive skills, she was overwhelmed by the variety of ways to describe what students needed to achieve deeper learning. "There's got to be an easier way," she thought. Her mind went to the applications on her phone, tools that help her get through her day, each represented by a simple image.

When she returned to Houston from the Network session, she brought the idea of matching the language with visuals to Houston's communications team, just like their weight-lifting brain. They came up with a variety of symbols, and the faculty chose four final images: hands linked for "teamwork and collaboration," an arrow and target for "precision and accuracy," a small figure pushing a large sphere for "persistence," and a head with an active, colorful brain for "complex reasoning strategies."

The icons, nicknamed APPs, have been made into posters and magnets. Teachers can slap a magnet or three up on the whiteboard next to the day's learning goal, telling the students exactly what they should be working on. The idea has spread beyond Cristo Rey Jesuit in Houston, and APPs are now showing up in classrooms—and work sites—throughout the Network.

The Cristo Rey Network common curriculum now incorporates two separate but related sets of knowledge and skills to promote deeper learning. "Thinking Practices," drawn from the Common Core math standard's eight practices, are embedded into all subject areas. The second set, captured in the APPs, are

"Lifelong Learning Behaviors." The Network also added two more APPs: a curvy road and compass for "initiative and self-direction," and an upward-trending graph for "productivity and accountability."

At Christ the King Preparatory School in Newark, Joseph Toma's U.S. history class is working on persistence, complex reasoning—including constructing support and analyzing perspectives—and teamwork and collaboration with a group project on social movements of the 1960s. While Conley's definition of key cognitive skills begins with formulating the problem, Toma lays out the structure for the project and questions they must answer. He even provides a list of important leaders and legislation for each movement, though he does not explain their importance. This is for the students to discover.

Toma books the computer lab for class, so that students can do online research on sites such as biography.com and UShistory.org. Sites that end with ".edu" are also a good option, the students say. The school also has a small library of donated books, categorized by a volunteer librarian. Christ the King wants to make sure its students know how to find physical books in a library and look up information in subscription databases before stepping into massive college libraries.

While students jot down notes from online sources in spiral notebooks, Toma circulates between groups, asking questions to make them dig further and move from collecting to analyzing and evaluating information: What were the differences between Martin Luther King Jr. and Malcolm X? What are their legacies today?

Each group eventually gave a twenty-minute presentation, with a time line and Prezi, a web-based tool that creates presentations that are like next-generation interactive PowerPoint slideshows. Through these presentations, students were expected to teach their classmates about the meaning and context of their movement.

Goettl calls such projects "minds-on learning," as opposed to simply "hands-on learning." Project-based learning has been proven to be an effective teaching strategy for engaging students on a deeper level than lectures. A project requires more than creating pretty presentations, though; students also must take deliberate steps that allow them to develop their cognitive abilities. Students learn the material while also learning how to do research, interpret information, and communicate their conclusions—essential skills of college-ready learners.

There is a drawback to project-based learning, though: such projects take a significant amount of time. Toma and his fellow history teachers across the Network could cover more material if they resorted to lecturing, but the students would not benefit from the process of discovering the material on their own. The increased engagement that comes with application ensures that students understand and retain new learning. With "fewer, clearer, and higher standards," the Cristo Rey Network curriculum focuses on depth more than breadth, Goettl says.

ASSESSMENT AND ADAPTATION

Just as D'Emma's students know the routine in her English class at Cristo Rey Philadelphia, Miguel Rios, the freshman at Verbum

Dei High School, knows what to do when he walks into his favorite class—science. He picks up his folder, a small whiteboard and marker, and a self-evaluation rubric.

The class is beginning a unit on subatomic particles, and after going through a lesson that includes a story about positive Patty Proton, neutral Nelly Neutron, and enraged Elliot Electron at the Nucleus Arcade, teacher Krista Frankovic asks a series of questions about the charge of an atom. If an atom loses or gains an electron, is it positive, negative, or neutral? With each question, the students write their answers down on their small whiteboards and, on command, lift them up and show her their answers. She quickly scans the room to see who gets the concept and who does not, then cold-calls on a student to explain. The response boards provide Frankovic and her students with immediate feedback, allowing her to monitor student understanding and adjust instruction.

There are great debates about the value of standardized testing in the education world, but "assessment" in a Cristo Rey school is a much broader idea than traditional tests. Using response boards to find out whether the whole class understands the charge of atoms is one example of an assessment that helps guide instruction. The math and science teachers at Verbum Dei have personalized Loyola Marymount University's Common Core Math and Science Teaching Program for the context of a Cristo Rey school. An essential element of the program is the use of ungraded quizzes to evaluate student learning. The quizzes, called "exit slips" when given at the end of the unit and "quick checks" when given a few weeks later, allow teachers to ensure initial and long-term understanding of concepts.

Frankovic hands back the class's last exit slip, testing the students on the idea of homogeneous and heterogeneous mixtures. Miguel has correctly labeled pictures of cereal and salad as heterogeneous and a glass of water as homogeneous, but his struggles with comprehension are evident. The exit slip asked him to "explain and justify" the answer with scientific language. Here Miguel struggled. After reviewing the right answer, Frankovic asks the students to give themselves a score based on a self-evaluation rubric. Miguel gives himself a 2.5 out of 4, which corresponds with "weak use" of science and math vocabulary.

The exit slips and quick checks allow the students to learn how to evaluate and monitor their own progress, a key college-level skill. Their grade is not based on these assessments, but from the beginning of the year students know that they will have a comprehensive end-of-course exam. Units are not simply facts to learn, regurgitate on a test, and then forget; they are part of a bigger story. One unit builds upon the previous one, just as the standards for sophomore year build upon the standards for freshman year. The Cristo Rey Network has developed end-of-course exams for its core classes to ensure that all of the classrooms are living up to the shared college-ready standards.

"If the test is a good test, it's okay to teach to it," Goettl explains. "If it represents what I want every one of my students to know and be able to do, that's beautiful. The test should be aligned to classroom learning and the curriculum standards." But assessment is only effective when teachers adapt instruction based on results. "The number-one purpose of assessment should be to drive classroom instruction," Goettl says.

Research on classroom instruction suggests that offering opportunities for group work, discussion, challenging tasks, and inquiry are promising methods of teaching, but researchers and educators still do not know how to help all students master core knowledge and skills.[19] "The education community has a lot to learn about how to meet the standards that policy rhetoric has set," write Tom Corcoran and Megan Silander of the Consortium for Policy Research in Education at Columbia University's Teachers College. "The point is for schools to take responsibility for each student and to try continually to do better."[20]

Teachers need to implement "adaptive instruction," Corcoran and Silander write. Teachers use the best practices, but adapt them as needed with real-time interventions based on assessments. "It is important to recognize that what is being 'adapted' in adaptive instruction is not the learning goals for students, but rather the instructional strategies and supports offered to help students reach the goals."[21]

Miguel's Algebra I math class is an example of how teachers can adapt to data on student achievement, personalizing education to the needs of individual students within a system of common standards. His teachers, Jessica Strains and Sarah Myers, combined their two classes after finding they had the same problem. Though each had small classes, they struggled to give students the help they needed because of the vast difference in math skills.

In the combined class, students start with a "do now" problem, simplifying a polynomial. Strains goes through another problem with the class while Myers checks in with individual students and encourages them to take notes. After her quick lesson, Strains gives a simple assessment. "Thumbs up, middle, or down. How are we doing?" she says, relying on the students' ability to monitor their own learning.

The class is all over the place. Miguel holds his thumb to the side—he gets it, but is still a little uncertain. As the class transitions into "active practice," Strains instructs the students with thumbs down to join her at the back table to go over the lesson again. Myers supervises the rest of the students working on a worksheet in pairs.

Miguel stays with the group working on the worksheet, which also allows for varying skill levels. Four rows of problems are divided into basic, proficient, and challenge questions. Miguel attempts a few proficient problems, but he also is distracted, talking about both math and football with his partner. He adds instead of subtracts and then tries to combine "8x" with "8." His partner shows him where he went wrong.

The homework also is divided into basic, proficient, and challenge problem sets. Myers asks Miguel how he is doing, and Miguel responds confidently. He should do the proficient level problem set for homework, then, she suggests. He backs down and says he will do the basic. Try the proficient problems, she encourages. Adapting to different ability levels does not mean letting a student off easily.

What Does Literacy Mean?

As Strains works her way through the math lesson with Miguel's class, she reminds the students that it is important not only to arrive at the right answer, but also to be able to explain how they got there. "Try to practice using that math vocabulary in your head because that's what we expect in your explanation," she instructs. Later, during active practice, Myers asks the student partners to explain to each other how to solve one of the equations. Just as he struggled to define types of mixtures on his exit slip in science class, he struggles to come up with the right words—such as "like terms," "polynomial," and "monomial"—to describe his work in math.

Miguel's struggles to communicate ideas are emblematic of a national issue. Students are not achieving literacy levels required for college. Less than half of ACT test takers met the college-ready reading benchmark, and literacy affects students' performance in all subjects.[22] Like the Common Core State Standards, the Cristo Rey standards include literacy in all classes, from math and science to religious and social studies and even visual and performing arts. "The teaching and assessment of college-ready reading and writing skills cannot be left to the English teacher alone," Goettl explains. These across-the-board efforts to increase literacy require six instructional shifts aligned with the Common Core:

1. A balance of literary and informational texts
2. Literacy across all content areas
3. Increasing complexity of texts
4. Text-based questions and answers
5. Writing using evidence
6. Academic vocabulary

For instance, Cristo Rey's math standards for Algebra I mandate that students be able to "identify the meaning of key terms in the context of one or more paragraphs of a mathematical text," requiring that teachers emphasize academic vocabulary in their lessons. Miguel and his classmates not only use the proper words in their head or with a partner, but they have to explain their answers on exit slips and tests. In their science class, Frankovic helps them break down and analyze the word "subatomic" to understand what the lesson is all about.

But reading is still rare in math and science at Verbum Dei—so rare that when Frankovic asks her students to read the story about the Nucleus Arcade, she makes note of the fact that they are reading. Verbum Dei students have textbooks for science and math at home, but they are merely used as reference books. The math department writes its own problem sets for homework.

Textbooks are sometimes not rigorous enough to meet the new standards of text complexity, Goettl says. The questions at the ends of chapters often do not require that a student support a response with evidence from the text, one of the goals of the instructional shifts. If students are to be ready to succeed as math and science majors in college, they need to be able to comprehend college-level textbooks and technical language.

Students' inability to read at grade level also affects college completion. According to the National Center for Education Statistics, students who need to take remedial reading classes in college are significantly less likely to earn a degree. In one study, only 30 percent of students who took remedial reading in a postsecondary program received a degree or certificate versus

69 percent of students who took no remedial course in their programs.[23]

The challenge is that once students fall behind in reading level, it is difficult to catch them back up. Differentiation of instruction sometimes has meant that a ninth-grade teacher with students who read at the fourth-grade level may only provide the students with fourth-grade level books, not allowing them to catch up to their instructional level. "While students do need to read text independently at their current reading level, they also need to have access, with teacher guidance, to complex texts at or above the grade level," Goettl says.

At a Cristo Rey school, freshmen are expected to read Shakespeare, even if they come into the school behind. Despite struggling with comprehension, Miguel says he enjoys Shakespeare's *Julius Caesar*. His English teacher, Ken Favell, starts the class with time to read, and Miguel opens a graphic novel version of *Julius Caesar* next to the original text, going back and forth to aid his understanding. After silent reading, the students want to restart an in-depth conversation from the day before about the theme of honor in the play. Studies have shown that high- and low-performing students who engage in dialogic instruction—free-flowing discussions where they can express opinions and ask questions—are better prepared to critique literary passages.[24]

Today, though, Favell guides the class into acting out a scene from the play. "I was Cassius last week," Miguel says with pride. The students have an assignment to write from the perspective of a particular character, giving them the opportunity to write from the text in a creative way. They enthusiastically choose to write as the characters they have played in class.

For the acting session, the students move their chairs to the back of the room, where two large camera lights illuminate their makeshift stage. Favell, who also runs a film club at the school, demonstrates a dramatic reading of Shakespeare by taking one part, while the students read their lines with little intonation. Favell occasionally has to leave character and return to being a teacher, taking a sleepy student's book, turning it to the right page, and handing it back to him. The boy starts following along with the rest of his classmates. Favell also pauses the reading to ask what difficult words mean and discuss a monologue. "Shakespeare," Favell says, "is meant to be heard and seen." He wants to give the students all the tools he can to aid comprehension, while still assigning challenging texts.

"Scaffolding"—extra supports such as the comic book and the class acting together—are necessary when students are not at grade level. "The scaffolding continues through sophomore, junior, and senior years, but each year it gets progressively less," Verbum Dei principal Dan O'Connell explains. "While they're here, we support them, but our goal is for our students to fly from the nest at graduation without our help."

There is a significant difference between what students read during their K–12 years and after. Students tend to read literary texts—novels, plays, or even narrative nonfiction. In higher education, work, or adult life in general, though, most reading materials are informational texts, such as news articles, memos, academic studies, and textbooks. The Common Core English Language Arts standards ask schools to better balance the types of texts teachers assign so that high-school graduates will be ready for a world of informational texts. By senior year of high school, 70 percent of reading materials should be informational texts.[25] Critics of the shift of balance between literary and informational texts argue that bus schedules and how-to manuals will replace the classics.[26] But the literacy benchmarks apply across disciplines. Students can still read Shakespeare in English if they are also reading the Gettysburg Address in history.

Aiming High

An increased emphasis on informational texts throughout their schooling should help students by the time they reach a class such as Advanced Placement U.S. Government. A class of Cristo Rey Boston seniors has just taken their AP test for U.S. Government—a useful exercise even if they do not score high enough to earn college credit, their teacher Carrie Wagner says.

Wagner started at North Cambridge Catholic before the school joined the Cristo Rey Network. As a young teacher, she thought it was a great place to be. Teachers believed they were doing a good job and explained away poor test scores. "Our students are not good test takers," they said.

Wagner was furious when she found out how poorly the school was serving its students. As a part of the effort to turn the school around, she and other teachers visited high-performing charter schools around Boston. At Match Charter School, students with the same demographics as North Cambridge Catholic students were mandated to take one Advanced Placement class during both their junior and senior years. "Why can't we do this?" Wagner thought.[27]

Six years later, a petite and very pregnant Wagner stands in front of her AP U.S. Government class. In a soft voice, she starts class with a classic prayer appropriate for the day after the AP test: "God, grant us the serenity to accept the things we cannot change, the courage to change the things we can, and the wisdom to know the difference." Then she instructs the students to give themselves a round of applause. Scores will come later. "But that's not what's important to me," she says. "You did college-level work. You can go into next year knowing that you can do college work."

These are not the best students in the class, she explains later. Those students take AP calculus or English. Even for the best students, though, their AP classes last two periods, so that teachers can provide more support. When Wagner assigns her last project for the AP class—a debate—she offers more guidance than one might expect in an AP class. She hands out a detailed research calendar and sample position papers modeling her expectations for the students.

Similar to the college-ready standards, requiring students to take AP classes necessitates that the whole school rise to the challenge. The journey to AP classes starts with the proficiency test freshman year, and recently the school has added a reading intervention for freshmen to help increase their comprehension levels before they reach Wagner's AP classroom. "Studies suggest that students who take an AP course are better prepared for college regardless of what score they get, and we want our students to be doing college-level work with us while we can still help them through it," Wagner says.

Sixteen of the twenty-three Cristo Rey schools with upperclassmen in the 2012–13 school year offered AP classes. Except for Spanish language and literature, in which Cristo Rey students excel, only 15 percent of AP test takers scored 3 or better on their tests.[28] Most of Wagner's students will not earn high enough scores on the AP test to qualify for college credit—typically a 3 on a 5-point scale. On practice tests, many scored a 1, but Wagner always looked to the data for encouragement—just five more correct answers and you will score a 2, she would tell a student. "Each step of the way, you have to find the way to give them hope, to give them a reason to keep working hard on it," she says. "That's my job, to get them through that."

Going through the process of an AP class can be beneficial for most students, regardless of their test score, Conley says. "The whole idea of a higher academic-challenge level gets us to the point that the content itself, heaven forbid, is not always the most important thing," he explains.[29] Even with a teacher who does not provide the guidance that Wagner does, students will discover key learning skills and techniques such as time management, study skills, persistence, and how to seek help on their own in high-level classes.

Even if they do not ace their AP tests, the students sitting in front of Wagner will be in college in the fall, and they will need these skills to succeed.

College Knowledge

According to Conley's model of college readiness, high-school students need to master one more area: "key transition knowledge and skills." College knowledge might be taken for granted in middle-class households, but students at Cristo Rey schools are often the first in their families to go to college. They have to learn terms such as "major," "minor," "liberal arts," "community college," "selectivity," "GPA," and "FAFSA" as if they were terms in a foreign language.

Nearly all schools have college-counseling seminars or classes for students. It is necessary to teach college knowledge during the school day, says Christopher Broughton, Cristo Rey Network's director of college initiatives. Putting it after school degrades its importance. It becomes "an extra thing instead of an essential thing," he says. The Network has created a basic standards document for college-counseling classes, but few resources or curricula exist for college counseling. The Network also is collecting extensive data on how its alumni perform in college from the National Student Clearinghouse. With this data and feedback from alumni, the Network plans to put together a college-counseling curriculum designed specifically to prepare low-income students for success in college.

At Verbum Dei, college guidance counselor Antoinette Bowie pulls underclassmen out of class six times a year for seminars about colleges and the application process. As a freshman, Miguel Rios is learning what success in high school looks like and why it is important for college admissions. He has learned to set personal and academic goals too. "If you really want to be successful, you're going to have to have goals and you're going to have to work for them," Miguel says. In his first quarter, he earned a 2.3 GPA. Since then he has met, then raised, his goal each quarter. He is aiming for a 3.0 by the end of his freshman year and a 3.5

for sophomore year. "If you set your goal too high, you will just be sad when you do not reach it," he says. "I try taking it step by step, quarter by quarter."

After the seminars, the students log on to Naviance, a web-based college guidance program that allows them to search careers, colleges, and majors. Career awareness is an essential piece of transition knowledge, but many low-income youth have a limited vision of career options; they think primarily of roles such as doctor, lawyer, musician, athlete, or teacher. Miguel, though, found civil engineering through Naviance. He has been looking for schools with civil engineering programs—and good basketball programs. Syracuse University is his most recent pick.

Young students tend to aim for familiarity over fit. Usually for Verbum Dei students, it is University of Southern California or UCLA. Christ the King students in Newark know about Princeton, and Cristo Rey Boston students shoot for Harvard and the University of Massachusetts. "They know these schools have good reputations, so that's where they want to go, but their desire to go to these schools might not be based on a lot of concrete facts," says Elizabeth Degnan, who heads the counseling programs at Cristo Rey Boston as principal for student life. "There's a lot of work in the beginning adjusting expectations and really identifying which schools are fit to each kid."

It is not bad to dream big, especially if it inspires students to rise to the occasion and do the work required to get into a top-tier school. Flora Baldwin, the college counselor at Christ the King in Newark, in fact, has all her students apply to their dream school, regardless of their qualifications. A gray-haired African-American woman, Baldwin remembers meeting her guidance counselor as a senior at a Newark public high school in the 1960s. "She sat me down at the desk, she looked at my file, and she said, 'Oh, you're not college material. You people are best at vocational jobs,'" Baldwin recalls. "I came out of there thinking I should be a college counselor, because I want to make sure that doesn't happen to somebody else." As if to spite her counselor, Baldwin went on to earn master's degrees in education and theological studies—she is also an assistant minister at her Baptist church.

To expose students to a large variety of schools, college counselors invite college representatives to visit and give presentations to small groups of students at lunch or after school. Christ the King hosts a college fair, while Bowie loads Verbum Dei's juniors into buses to take them to a college fair in Pasadena, twenty miles north of the school. But for understanding the norms and culture of college life, nothing beats visiting a university. A number of students participate in special summer immersion programs designed to introduce students from low-income communities to college life. For most students, local colleges provide the best opportunity to see what college campuses are like.

Even if they are not the best options, students are often attracted to local colleges for logical and emotional reasons. Public schools may have low in-state tuitions, and students see the cost benefit of staying at home. Low-income and first-generation college students also may fear the unknown and feel more comfortable staying close to family, says Martinique Starnes, who leads personal, college, and alumni counseling as Verbum Dei's dean of counseling and student affairs. They and their parents may not have role models who have gone away to college and stayed connected to their families.

Pablo Cabrera, for instance, graduated from Verbum Dei in 2013. He applied to four California State University system schools because of their low in-state tuition and a state grant for low-income students. Although he applied to two schools in northern California, he chose Cal State Dominguez Hills, an easy commute from his home. He is close to his family, and his grandfather, whom he considers a father figure, is on dialysis and needs extra care. The six-year completion rate for the college, though, is only 25 percent.[30]

"The college decision-making process has a lot of moving parts, one of which is the emotions of a seventeen-year old," says college completion expert Joseph Yeado, of the Education Trust. "The more that school counselors can try to impart data, the more it will help students and their families make informed decisions."

It is essential, Yeado says, to look not only at the requirements to get into the school, but also at what the school is doing to help young people graduate from college, such as mandatory advising, new-student orientation, freshman learning communities, and opportunities to work with faculty on research. Students who live on campus, work while in school (though no more than fifteen hours), or take fifteen credits per semester are more likely to graduate from college on time as well. Large unmet financial needs— tuition not covered by loans or grants— also correlate with low college completion rates.

"Money is almost always the number-one factor for students in their college decisions," Cristo Rey Boston's Degnan says. She advises students and their parents to keep their unmet need as low as possible. Students will usually have $5,500 in subsidized federal loans each year, and for Boston's class of 2013 the average unmet need was about $2,000, less than the full tuition for Cristo Rey Boston (though few pay full tuition at Cristo Rey schools). Some students disregard the school's advice and go to schools they cannot afford, Degnan says. Although they may make it through one or two years, they often end up unable to pay tuition one semester. They miss registration and have to extend their college experience, making it more expensive in the long run.

College counselors can also point students to the forty-plus University Partners that the Network has formed. University Partners often give generous financial-aid packages to Cristo Rey students, along with a holistic review of their application. The schools provide support programs to Cristo Rey graduates who enroll as well.

Georgetown University, the most elite University Partner, has enrolled sixty-four Cristo Rey graduates, and it has yet to lose one student. "Our overall dropout rate is not zero percent, so it's a higher-than-average persistence rate," says Melissa Foy, executive director of the Georgetown Scholarship Program. "Cristo Rey students are uniquely resilient and able to overcome challenges and obstacles."

Cristo Rey alumni at Georgetown were at the top of their high-school classes, but it is not just the best students who do well in college. Cristo Rey students persist in college at rates similar to those in the highest income bracket. There is something more in them that is not revealed by AP and ACT test scores. What helps them both go to and succeed in college may come from Cristo Rey's secret sauce: the corporate work-study program.

CHAPTER FIVE

A Work-Program Revolution

Miguel Rios comes to Verbum Dei High School on a Friday dressed to impress, his usual white and black uniform spiced up with pinstripe pants and a dark red button-down shirt with a crisp collar. As he does every day, he wears a thin black tie and shiny loafers, and his short black hair is lightly greased and combed forward.

His theology teacher is waiting at the door to a multipurpose room, where students check in before being sent out to work at companies around the city. When his teacher asks him for an essay, he apologizes sheepishly and says he forgot to print it, then shuffles into the room.

At the check-in, work-study director Cristina Cuellar-Villanueva reminds the freshman boys that their second semester performance reviews would be coming up in the next month.

Then Cuellar-Villanueva brings up a more sensitive subject: facial hair. She makes light of the clumps of hair that have started appearing on the fourteen- and fifteen-year-old boys' faces. "It's not cute, it's not professional," she says to giggles. "If some girl tells you it's cute, tell her Ms. V. says, 'No, it isn't.'" A tall young Latina from Watts, Ms. V., as she is known around school, talks with students with a sense of authority, but also familiarity. Turning serious, she suggests that there are plenty of people on campus who could teach them how to shave if they do not have somebody at home to help them.

Miguel is the man of his house, but his mustache is hardly ready for a razor. Still, Cuellar-Villanueva does not have to worry about the way Miguel looks or acts at work. Despite his struggles in the classroom, Miguel shines at work. "He knows what to say and when to say it," Cuellar-Villanueva says. "It's genuine. It's not him trying to impress people. That's just who he is."

Even if he keeps forgetting to turn in his theology paper, Miguel is thoughtful about the movie he was supposed to write about— the story of a boy who is an unlikely hero. He likes Verbum Dei, even though it is an all-boys school. The corporate work-study program is one of his favorite parts. "I like hard work," he says. "I don't like to be lazy. I like being active and doing something that makes me better, that helps me become a better man, so that I can help my family, my mom especially."

Miguel's slick exterior hides a tough home life. His mom is raising him and three younger sisters on her own and without a job. He managed to remain in Catholic school on scholarships and is on the free-lunch program at Verbum Dei. Even though his little sisters get on his nerves, he tries to be a role model for them. "When I'm at school and I feel lazy, I think about my sisters," he says. "I want to show them you have to keep trying. Everything you want to accomplish you have to work for."

Cuellar-Villanueva dismisses the students by carpool assignment, and the students head to a fleet of vans that carry them in all directions around the Los Angeles metropolitan area. Miguel is in the last and largest group, which takes what looks like a retrofitted public bus to work sites downtown.

When the bus arrives there, eleven miles north of the school, Miguel gets off at one of the first stops with four friends who work nearby. They walk to the corner, and with a formality odd for young teenagers, they shake hands stiffly before turning toward their own buildings. On most days, they will come back together for lunch—meeting up at a nearby food court to talk sports and compare their jobs. There is competition for who has the best work site, Miguel says. He thinks he has one of the best.

It is only 8:30 A.M., but Miguel is ready to get to work. He enters one of the buildings operated by his work sponsor, Brookfield Properties, shaking hands with the security guard in a large marble atrium. He nods to the others in the elevator—also lined with marble—and swipes his official badge, selecting the twenty-second floor. After a few stops, the doors open, and he steps out into a white marble entry hall with large images on the walls showing the buildings that Brookfield Properties owns across the world. Through the glassed-in conference room across the reception area, the Los Angeles skyline shines.

The office is quiet at this time in the morning, but Miguel

greets everyone politely, granting the same respect to security guards and office workers. His supervisor is out, so the receptionist gives him his list of assignments. He will not be able to meet his friends for lunch. He will be sitting in on a lunch meeting with some company executives. Before he gets into his more substantive work, the receptionist asks him to stock the refrigerator with water and soda for the meeting. Miguel takes off his jacket and rolls up the sleeves of his dress shirt, just as he does in the classroom. Even if he rarely understands what is going on in meetings, he takes pride in preparing for them. He likes the fact that his supervisors tell him they depend on him, even for a simple assignment. "It shows that they actually care about us," he says.

It is a big help to have Miguel around, says receptionist Amanda Kullman. She has Miguel working on a data entry project this morning, adding the dates from certificates of insurance to a database. Even though she has to take the time to show him what to do, having Miguel do the task frees her up to focus on other work. Miguel gets to work, pointing carefully to the form on the paper to make sure he is entering the right information. He squints his eyes and leans in toward the computer screen. "Should have brought my glasses today," he mumbles to himself.

For most students, communication is the biggest challenge at work. Talking with adults is intimidating for most fourteen-year-olds, and the office is a new environment for them. Parents of Cristo Rey students generally do not work in corporate America, and many of the students have never left their own neighborhood. When adults from the schools go out with freshmen to help them find their offices for the first time, even boisterous teens get quiet and wide-eyed in the elevator, later revealing that they had never ridden one before. It is not surprising that in a foreign environment, students would be reluctant to engage in small talk or ask questions when they are unclear on an assignment.

Miguel has never had that problem, office manager Barbara Caples says. "He was not shy from day one—at all. He's great. He's got a smile on his face 24/7."

Rather than shy away from feedback, Miguel sought it out, asking Caples to go over his mid-year review with him. During her eight years as a Cristo Rey supervisor, Miguel was the first student to ask her for a review. "I thought that was really commendable. He wants to improve," Caples says.

Caples encouraged him with praise and suggested that he develop his computer skills, the other big challenge for Cristo Rey students. She has developed manuals to help student workers better learn programs like Excel and Outlook. They receive training at school as well, but Cristo Rey students come to work with various levels of comfort with technology. Miguel, who does not have a computer at home, struggles with typing. Some students only access the Internet on their phone, and their experience with a keyboard may be limited to typing with their thumbs. "You kind of expect them to know it, and they don't," Caples says of the technology skills.

Though they are in a grown-up environment, some of the Cristo Rey students are still fourteen-year-olds. Miguel has a lot of room for growth, but Cuellar-Villanueva says, "He sees the light at the end of the tunnel, and he's like, 'I'm getting there.'"

How It Works

Miguel's experience at work is typical for Cristo Rey freshmen. Sending students to work started as a brilliant funding mechanism for a Catholic school, but administrators soon realized that working was a learning experience for the students as well. The work-study program became the "secret sauce" of the Cristo Rey school by reinforcing the high expectations of the classroom and expanding students' vision of their potential.

Students are attracted to the schools because they get a chance to work, while corporate sponsors love the opportunity to fill an entry-level position with a reliable worker and help shape students who will someday become part of the workforce.

"It's rewarding for me," says Caples. "I like getting to know the kids. You take them from a freshman to a senior, and the growth is just amazing."

The setup of the program is essentially the same at all Cristo Rey schools. The work-study office functions as a separate non-profit job-placement company within each school. It is responsible for training the students and filling out all of the appropriate paperwork to confirm that students are legally employable. The work-study department places students at companies, charging them an annual fee that varies based on the local market. Four students make up a team equivalent to one full-time employee at an average cost of $28,000, including benefits and withholding taxes.[1]

Freshmen work on one day, sophomores the next, and so on, with the four students taking turns to cover the fifth day of the week. In all, students will be at work five days a month. They take on entry-level assignments, such as data entry, filing, or reception work, though upperclassmen may take on more complex projects depending on their skills and interests.

When they apply to the school, students—and parents—frequently ask when they will see their first paycheck. The parents and students, however, agree to assign the wages to the school, which uses them to pay for the school's operating expenses. When the school is at capacity, more than half of operating cash revenue should come from the work-study program. If the school is not at capacity, its cost per student will be higher, as many of the costs of educating children—the facility, administration, faculty, and support staff—are fixed. As a new school adds students, operating costs should not rise drastically, but each new student will bring in more revenue.

The work-study program sends a fourth of a school's student body off campus each day. The school must transport students to their jobs on time and safely. In a city like Los Angeles, that means running a fleet of vans and buses to job sites. It can take an hour to get to some sites. In cities like Boston or New York, that means sending students on public transportation to reach their work sites—and convincing concerned parents that they will be okay on their own. If a student gets sick at work, work-study staff can be pulled away at a minute's notice to go pick the student up.

Students work on the same day as their classmates, and classes are organized in blocks so that they do not meet on the day that the students are working. The constraint on the schedule means that school days are longer and there is less room for electives. If students are at work until 4:30 or 5:00, they also are not able to participate in after-school activities that day. If their sports team has a game, they miss it. The class schedule requires greater self-discipline, as students must remember that their essay still needs to be turned in, even if they are going to work. They may have to take a test on Wednesday, even if they are working on a Tuesday.

In the end, the students, faculty, and parents make do with these inconveniences because of the revenue the jobs bring in and the impact they have on students. The work program is a critical part of the students' educational experience.

Why It Works

On the most immediate level, students can see how some of their classroom studies are relevant in the working world. Miguel, for instance, used math to work with spreadsheets in the accounting department at Brookfield Properties, even finding an error, he says with pride. Grammar is important not just in papers for teachers, but also in e-mails to supervisors and coworkers.

Miguel does not need to read Shakespeare or know calculus to do data entry or filing, but when entering information from certificates of insurance, he does need to be precise and accurate, one of the lifelong learning behaviors emphasized in Cristo Rey classrooms. The work-study program reinforces these skills, which researchers have found to be one of the keys to achievement.

Some schools have even experimented with bringing the APPs, visual tools for lifelong learning behaviors, to the workplace. Though supervisors are not trained as teachers, "the fundamentals of the APPs resonate," says Dan Walsh, the corporate work-study director at the Houston school, where the APPs were developed for teachers. Words like "precise and accurate," "teamwork and collaboration," and "persistence" are as applicable in the work environment as they are in the classroom. Schools are developing ways to help supervisors use the symbols when assigning a student a project and evaluating the student's performance.

Much of the research into work-based learning experiences confirms that such programs improve these "soft skills," in business parlance. The Search Institute, which studies what students need to be successful, compiled a report for the Cristo Rey Network that outlines the results of research on work-based learning programs for disadvantaged high-school students. Though the research is thin, studies of federally funded school-to-work programs "paint a promising picture," the report says. Work-based learning experiences resulted in improved interpersonal skills (especially with adults), planning and decision-making skills, personal responsibility, leadership, confidence, self-concept, and even physical health, among other positive qualities. Students who participated in these programs were more committed to learning and had an increased sense of "work hope," which the Search Institute describes as the motivational levels to overcome obstacles to success.

The definition of "work hope" mirrors what University of Pennsylvania psychologist Angela Duckworth calls "grit" and what Catholic schools call "character." Grit is the passion and persistence to work toward long-term goals despite obstacles. Students with grit, Duckworth has found, are the ones who do best in school. It is not surprising, then, that the studies on work programs show that participants had better GPAs, attendance, student retention rates, academic course completion, and on-time graduation, though not standardized tests.[2] Cristo Rey Boston attributes the increase in the number of graduates enrolling in college after it became a Cristo Rey school to the confidence the students found at work. Only 29 percent of the class of 2004 enrolled in college, but 69 percent of the class of 2007, which had experienced the Cristo Rey program for three years, did so.[3]

Just as sending a low-income child to a Catholic school will not guarantee academic success, sending a student to a workplace does not guarantee that a teen will become a confident and responsible leader. The Search Institute found that programs need to connect work to the classroom, involving teachers and parents. There also must be clear instructions and expectations for both students and employers, as well as mentor relationships at work.[4]

A student does not need to become close with his supervisor, Miguel says. He showed Caples his usual charm by wishing her a happy Mother's Day, she says, while she asks how school is going. Simple questions—"What's your favorite class?"—reinforce the importance of education. Asking what colleges students want to go to or what they want to be when they grow up keeps them focused on long-term goals.

Outside of school, students might not have adults at home or in their communities asking them questions that require that they think about the future. Parents may be too worried about what they will be able to feed their children for dinner to focus on where their children will be in four years. Working among successful college-educated professionals expands students' vision of what they are capable of, giving students like Miguel an incentive to work hard in school. "Being surrounded by certain people, you want to be like them," Miguel says.

At Brookfield Properties, the Verbum Dei students have an office with a view of downtown. The desk is clean other than a computer. Yearbooks from the past four years of Verbum Dei and a picture of this year's four-person student team are the only items on the shelf. Caples laughs that she has just a cubicle, while they have an office, though the student workers do have to give it up every once in a while when employees from other cities have business in Los Angeles.

Having an office makes Miguel feel special. "That's what stood out to me on the first day," he says. "I went home and told my mom."

As he looks out of his office window, Miguel points out where his friends work and shares which buildings are his favorites. He prefers the older architectural style with intricate brick and concrete work. Far below where he works, he points to rooftop patios with pools and spaces for weddings. Next door, a building is being torn down floor by floor, revealing a tangle of rebar, concrete, and steel. A new building will be on its way up when he comes back to work next fall, Miguel says. A builder himself, he is fascinated by the construction site. Recently, he had built a shelf and figured out how to make his own basketball hoop out of a board, bike tire rim, and netting.

When he started at Cristo Rey, he told people he wanted to go to University of North Carolina for college because former NBA star Michael Jordan went to school there. But then he started to do career research and decided he would like to become a civil engineer so that he can build things for a living. Now he wants to go to Syracuse University in New York. It has both a good basketball team and a good civil engineering program, he explains.

Besides his desire to build, he found in his research that civil engineers are often in leadership positions. Although his office is nice, he has seen the corner offices at work. "I don't want to have a boss. I want to be the boss," he says.

If he wants to be the boss, Miguel knows that he will have to stay focused and work hard. The last time he was at work, Brookfield Properties had made the front page of the *Los Angeles Times* because it had entered into a merger agreement and acquired four buildings downtown. It was now the largest landlord in downtown Los Angeles.

Miguel was not exactly clear on the details of the deal, but he was impressed. He saw his future in the company's achievement—he saw it as a story of "wanting more than you're supposed to have." Brookfield Properties can become the largest landlord in downtown LA, and he can graduate from high school, go on to college, and become a civil engineer at the top of a company. You work hard for something you want, and you can achieve it, he says.

A PROFESSIONAL DEVELOPMENT PROGRAM FOR STUDENTS

From the day he walked into Verbum Dei, Miguel was asking the right questions, Cuellar-Villanueva says. Most fourteen-year-olds, though, do not initially understand what they have signed up for when they enroll in a Cristo Rey school. To prepare them to enter the workforce and represent their school well, each school provides a summer program for incoming freshmen.

The incoming freshmen at Verbum Dei have barely finished celebrating eighth-grade graduation when they start their high-school careers at the end of June. On the first day of work-study training, called SOAR (Summer Opportunity for Academic and Employment Readiness) at Verbum Dei, about 130 boys stand quietly in two single-file lines in the courtyard of the outdoor campus to check in. They wear shiny black loafers, black pants, and a black tie. Many of their white shirts have fresh creases in the sleeves, having been put on for the first time that morning. They pick up their schedules and name tags, then the boys—some of them less than five feet tall—return to their parents waiting on the sides. When it is time for the day to begin, they file silently into the multipurpose room and take a seat in rows of white folding chairs. Only when a teacher gives them permission to talk do they whisper with one another.

Some come with a small group of other boys from a Catholic grammar school. Others come from public school, not knowing another person in the class. Principal Dan O'Connell greets them, saying they are brothers now, but at lunch some boys sit alone. For the most part, they are typical teenagers on the first day of high school, dealing with the usual social pressures along with a barrage of placement tests to see where their math and Spanish skills stand. But at Verbum Dei, they are also assessed on their ability to alphabetize names as if they were putting files away for a company and to rewrite an e-mail starting with "Wuz up?" so that it is professional.

At most Cristo Rey schools, the summer training program takes place in the two weeks before school starts, but Verbum Dei's program is four weeks at the beginning of the summer. Unlike the Network academic program, the curriculum for the work-study training is looser. Still, the skills students learn are generally the same at all Cristo Rey schools—hard skills such as Outlook, Excel, and filing systems, and soft skills such as making small talk and maintaining direct eye contact. Students also learn about labor laws and discrimination and find out how to resolve conflicts with supervisors and coworkers.

On the first day of SOAR, Cuellar-Villanueva stands at the library door to greet each student lined up outside. "Good morning. How are you?" she says, extending her hand to shake the students' hands. This will be the routine in all classes for the rest of the summer program. Teachers expect a firm handshake, eye contact, and a proper greeting. But today most students make eye contact just briefly before looking down. "I'm good," many say shyly, already halfway to a chair.

"That's a break-your-hand-off type of handshake!" Cuellar-Villanueva says to one overcompensator. But generally the boys take her hand too lightly. "No wet noodles," she explains later when she has them practice handshakes, breaking down how one hand should fit into the other.

In class, the main order of the day is introductions, but the introductions serve a greater purpose than learning names. One of the first boys announces that his unique quality is that he likes video games. "Who else likes video games?" Cuellar-Villanueva asks. They all raise their hands and, to groans, Cuellar-Villanueva bans anybody else from saying so. When a boy at the first table slouches and mumbles his name while his arms swing awkwardly at his side, Cuellar-Villanueva makes him repeat his introduction. His eye roll does not go unnoticed. One student says he does not like math. "Then we cannot be friends," Cuellar-Villanueva jests in response. She perks up when other students say they like history, reading, or science.

"I'm not impressed by some of you," she warns, asking the students to analyze their classmates' introductions. Students share that confidence and humor left good impressions—unless somebody was trying too hard to be funny. "I love science, too," a boy offers, pointing to a classmate who had used his love of science as his unique characteristic. "Good, so commonalities," Cuellar-Villanueva says.

"First impressions are . . ." Cuellar-Villanueva says, getting the students to complete her sentence. "Lasting impressions," they respond.

The work-study training, Cuellar-Villanueva explains to the boys, is a four-week interview. One of the reasons the summer training program is four weeks long at Verbum Dei is so that work-study staff can get to know the boys better. For the first few weeks, they tend to be quiet and well-behaved, if a little uncertain, but after a few weeks they start feeling comfortable at the school and come out of their shells.

In the lesson on small talk a few weeks into SOAR, they will feel free to joke during a serious discussion of inappropriate questions to ask their supervisors. "What color is your underwear?" one boy chimes in after others suggest religion and home problems as off-limit topics at work. "That's harassment, buddy," Cuellar-Villanueva laughs, using the joke as a segue to discuss other topics of conversation that could be harassment.

Misbehavior is not typically the problem with small talk at work. "One-word answers! That's what the supervisors are complaining about," Cuellar-Villanueva exclaims when a student answers only "yes" in a practice conversation. It is not just them, she explains to the class. The Network surveyed corporate sponsors from all the schools and found that communication is the number-one issue that employers want the students to work on. They are great kids—hardworking and polite—supervisors report, but they are so quiet at first.

As they become more comfortable at school, misbehavior sometimes becomes a problem. At the end of week two, the school makes six calls home to parents. "If we cannot get through to you by talking to your parents, it's going to be a hard year for you here," says Mashanda Finn, who can be stern with students one minute and laughing with them the next. As a corporate work-study program coordinator during the year, she serves as principal during the summer training. Forming relationships with parents or guardians so that they and the school are on the same team is critical to shaping the teens into workers, she says.

On the final Friday of SOAR, work supervisors come to the school for a job fair. Students have the chance to shake potential employers' hands, show off their new small-talk skills, and pass on a résumé developed in computer class. There will still be holes in their computer skills and confidence, but after just four weeks they will be well on their way to becoming Verbum Dei gentlemen.

CONTINUING EDUCATION

At the end of the summer training, the school matches students with corporations, taking into account both parties' preferences. They want the companies to be happy, but they also want the students to be excited about their work.

For Miguel, Cuellar-Villanueva saw that his and Caples's personalities would match well and that Brookfield Properties would keep him busy. "Brookfield requires the students to be independent, and he exhibited those skills in the summer training. We were able to make that match," she explains.

Still, work is not exactly what most students expect. They have a glamorized image of work from TV, Cuellar-Villanueva says. At Verbum Dei, positions at Sony Pictures Entertainment are highly coveted, but the jobs are no more exciting than any other job. "When they're in the human resource office, and they're stuck there assisting with filing and data entry, and they thought they were going to meet Will Smith and Drake and all these movie stars, then they're discouraged," she says. Even students in more run-of-the-mill industries think they will do more. They see themselves sitting in a fabulous office, making phone calls and talking to people, maybe running out to Starbucks to get coffee for their supervisor.

"We have to keep them motivated and reassure them that they're going to school so they don't end up in a job where what they're doing is filing all day," Cuellar-Villanueva says. "We want them to have the corner office." She explains to the students, "School is what we do because we don't want to end up in a mediocre job. We're better than that."

Some schools have students switch jobs every year, giving them a variety of corporate experiences and connections. Others, including Verbum Dei, encourage students to stay at the same company for all four years. If they stay at least two years, Cuellar-Villanueva explains, they build connections that can lead to letters of recommendation and potential future jobs. They can be trained further and take on more complex projects. The return on investment for the companies is stronger too, when they do not have to retrain new students every year.

Cristo Rey St. Martin College Prep in Waukegan, Illinois, maintains a "book of jobs" to describe the wide-ranging projects that the high-school student workers take on. Even filing and data-entry projects are substantial; student workers handle vast quantities of confidential information and check databases to ensure that information is accurate. Students also help companies put the data to use, creating reports in Excel and preparing information for audits.

Multiple organizations use students as translators, including for client meetings. Marketing departments have students conducting customer, competitor, and other market research online. Research can be technical—trademark infringements for a brand management company's legal department and genetic differences between populations for a pharmaceutical company. Some students have the opportunity to develop their creativity working with graphics applications. In many IT departments, student workers work on company computers, updating software and licenses and even providing IT support to graduate students at a university. Supervisors are often surprised to find out how much the students can do.

Issues with student workers are rare, but when they do happen, they tend to follow a pattern. Each year has its challenges. Freshmen tend to be eager to please, but shy and nervous. As students become more comfortable, they might start testing boundaries. They may use their cell phone at work or come back from their lunch break ten minutes late, wondering if anyone will notice. By senior year, a few students lose motivation, or they may become overconfident and make silly mistakes. Most problems are handled at work, as they would be with any employee. For small discipline issues, a quick call back to the work-study office usually keeps students in check. Just as it is important for parents and the school to be on the same team for disciplinary issues, students need to see that there is clear communication between work supervisors and the school. If a problem continues, the school will bring parents in and create a plan to help the student improve.

The work-study team has little time to train the students as a group beyond the summer program, and the Network has just begun to develop a Network work-study curriculum for all four years. Check-in at the beginning of each day provides just a few minutes to share general reminders—about facial hair or evaluations, for instance. Some schools hold work-study classes once a week during a study block, repeating topics from the summer training.

In Houston, work-study skills are reinforced in a half-credit "college- and career-readiness class." The class continues through all four years, culminating in the college application process senior year. Freshmen learn study skills, but they also read *The 7 Habits of Highly Effective Teens*—which other schools teach as part of the summer work-study training program. The sophomore-year program has been tweaked to include more technical skills—typing, Excel, e-mailing—which are important both for college and for their job performance now.

Outside of the class, they approach further training as "individual enrichment" based on work supervisors' requests. "We pride ourselves on a rapid-response, customer-service mentality," Walsh says. If a supervisor wants a student to become more comfortable typing, the work-study program will fit practice time in, even if it is at 5:00 P.M., after all the day's activities are done. Getting students to stay late is about positioning, Walsh explains. "We're excited that your work-study sponsor thinks highly of you and thinks you're ready to do even more," he will tell students. "We want to position you for success."

Verbum Dei has a rigorous job skills training program beyond the summer program. Throughout their four years, students must complete independent assignments from a series of books to be turned in to the work-study staff monthly. Each year, the book and assignment match the challenges of their stage in high school; freshmen review *Business Skills Exercises,* the same book they used during the summer training. The book has exercises on time management, answering phones, postage, and typing. At first they do not want to do the work on their own, says Cuellar-Villanueva. "But when they see it at work, they're like, 'Oh, we talked about this,' or 'This was part of our homework assignment. This is actually real.' They start to see the connection."

As sophomores, students focus on workplace ethics. They are presented with scenarios, which they often recognize from work, and learn how to confront them. Junior year focuses on business math, such as percentages and stocks, while seniors use a book called *On Your Own* to learn life skills—reading a bank statement, living on their own, and interviewing for jobs. Students also must update their résumé every semester and complete a writing assignment ranging from a company history to a business plan. As seniors, they put together a portfolio containing their résumé, performance reviews, certificates, and awards.

Every school has supervisors evaluate their students, and many assign grades and grant awards for being a stellar student worker. Students frequently are motivated by more than praise. Some work sponsors hire students over the summer as interns, and when they do, students can take home their paycheck.

The vast majority of students meet or exceed the expectations of their supervisors. In Houston, 93 percent of students are at that level. "The human-resource executives I work with have said, 'Dan, if I could get 93 percent success from my employee base, I'd be pretty happy,'" Walsh says. "I've come to learn that's a pretty darn good score. Being the A-type players that we are, we want 100 percent, so we spend a lot of time on the 7 percent."

If summer work is the carrot, there is also a stick: students can be fired from their jobs. On rare occasions, behavior will be so egregious that the school will expel a student, such as if a student steals from the workplace. But generally students get in trouble at work for not following directions, doing their jobs poorly, or having a bad attitude.

Walsh divides his 7 percent into two categories based on the cause of the problem: aptitude and attitude. The former can be handled with after-school remediation, but the latter is more difficult. "That issue is probably at the core, 'Do you really want to be here? Are you open to growth?'" Walsh says. If the problem cannot be resolved through cooperation between the supervisor, school, and parents, the school will pull the students from their jobs.

Ten percent of students at Cristo Rey schools are placed in non-profit organizations to serve as a "bench" of workers who can be called on to fill in for students who have been fired. Strong workers are kept on the nonprofit bench because they can easily step into a company spot where another student has faltered.

Fired students, meanwhile, enter a retraining program for a month or more to prepare them for a new job. While their classmates head to work, they stay behind at school and work on job-skills assignments. They often read *The 7 Habits of Highly Effective Teens,* write a book report on it, and write letters of apology to their supervisor, school, and parents. Schools want to be sure they understand what went wrong and how to avoid it before placing them back into a work environment. They have a second chance, but that is all. After being fired twice, a student will be asked to leave Cristo Rey. On average, one or two students a year may be expelled because of work problems.[5]

Tying their tuition to work is key for the students, says Preston Kendall, the original work-study director at the Cristo Rey Jesuit in Chicago and now president of Cristo Rey St. Martin in Waukegan. The work-study program would not be as effective as a voluntary internship at a public school. "If you can lose your job, you're going to treat it seriously," he says. "Part of the magic for us is that the kids know it's real."

TRAINING THE ADULTS

On the first day that the original school in Chicago sent students to work, Kendall was nervous. He and Father John Foley, the school's president, expected corporations to call, wanting to send the students back to the school. Instead, when they did call Kendall on that first day, it was to thank the school for sending the students to them.[6]

Since that day, corporate sponsors have been largely satisfied with the Cristo Rey program. Of the students with completed end-of-year reviews in 2012, 95 percent met or exceeded expectations, and the average renewal rate for corporate sponsors was 87 percent. At the Chicago school—which has relationships that go back to 1996—97 percent of corporate sponsors renewed.[7] Students provide a school with its best advertising, but corporate work-study directors also work hard to maintain relationships with the companies. They constantly have to recruit more corporate sponsors to replace those that do not renew and to find more jobs for students.

Corporate work-study directors often connect to executives at new companies through school board member introductions. Increasingly, they are also using their national Network, finding connections through other schools. Typically, the decision to hire a team of Cristo Rey students comes from the higher-ups in a company. The work-study director may appeal to a CEO's faith or sense of justice, but the schools also sell their "product"—the students—as a smart business decision.

Students are not hired as charity. Early on, the founders of Cristo Rey found that a work-study job funded through a company's operation budget was more likely to be renewed than a job funded through a company's charitable foundation. Work-study directors sell their teams of high-school students as being more reliable and cheaper than the temporary or entry-level employees usually hired to complete projects and basic office work. The average daily work attendance for students is 97.9 percent across the Network—and students have to make up days they miss.[8]

Although a CEO may love the idea of giving low-income teens the opportunity to succeed, the supervision of the student workers is typically passed down to office workers. Some, like Barbara Caples at Brookfield Properties, embrace the role, while others look at supervising students as another task on their to-do list. Caples admits it takes a lot of her time, which is why she rotates the students to different departments. "If you take it seriously, it's a big responsibility," she says. "You don't want these kids coming and just wasting their time by giving them busy work. You really want them to get something out of the program."

"It's important that our students are treated fairly, similarly if not exactly like any employee," Cuellar-Villanueva says. That means that students should not be treated like charity cases—it does the students no good to let them off easy with little to do or to rate them highly on evaluations if they are not deserving of the praise. At the same time, they should not be let go without proper warnings and interventions. If the students hear "good job" at the end of the day, they will take it to heart, even if their evaluations do not meet expectations, Cuellar-Villanueva explains.

To avoid any such miscommunications, work-study staff build strong relationships not only with CEOs, but also with the students' supervisors. Part of the selling point for companies is that their employees will be trained in how to supervise the students.

Schools hold new supervisor trainings and thank-you luncheons. Some schools match new supervisors with experienced clients, so they can find out how another company uses the students. Others send out newsletters with best practices and unique projects that students are doing—everything from wearing scrubs and wheeling around patients after operations at a hospital to working in cash disbursement at a bank where $40 million pass through each day.

The corporate work-study departments also want their clients to understand that they can call the school at any point for help. When Anthony Caldwell took over the work-study program at Christ the King in Newark, New Jersey, he instituted monthly calls to corporate sponsors to check in. "I want to be proactive if there's any type of situation going on in the workplace, that we address it immediately and not let it go," Caldwell says. His program manager, Brenda Pescoran, the older sister of two Christ the King students, has worked at the school since it launched and knows some clients so well that she greets them with a hug.

Most of the time, their check-in calls are positive. But if there is an issue, Caldwell or Pescoran can go out and meet with the students and supervisors to address them. The school's responsiveness has helped them retain work sponsors, and when word spread among the students that the work-study department was watching, the students were less tempted to be late or use their cell phones at work. "Our kids are good kids, but kids are kids," Caldwell says.

Dave Roberts, the corporate work-study director at Cristo Rey Boston, owned a boutique staffing company before starting at Cristo Rey. Even with his experience, client relations can be a challenge. In the business world, eight to ten clients would generate $3 million, Roberts points out, but at the school it takes 105 active clients to generate that revenue.

In his first months on the job, he set a goal to visit each client four times during the year. During site visits, he has clients take him through a "day in the life" of a student worker for a detailed account of the day. Learning from a colleague at Cristo Rey St. Martin, he is putting together a job book that he hopes will help prospective clients see what students are capable of. "They can do a lot of things. It's just that you have to identify that work," he says.

Investing in the Future

For many corporate sponsors, the Cristo Rey work-study program is an investment in the future, a training ground for tomorrow's diverse workforce.

Christ the King in Newark struggled to find corporate sponsors in its first years, as Newark is a small city with great poverty. Still, some of its corporate sponsors stand out for understanding the importance of the program not only for the students, but also for themselves. Much of it has to do with a corporation's culture, says June Inderwies, board chair of the school and a corporate sponsor.

Inderwies is executive director and COO of Gibbons P.C., a mid-size Atlantic region law firm. Its namesake, Judge John Gibbons, instilled in the firm the value of giving back. The firm hires two associates every year to focus on pro bono cases, and it participates in other educational opportunities to expose disadvantaged students to the practice of law. It also takes a chance on people, giving them the opportunity to succeed, Inderwies says, pointing to herself as an example. She started working at the firm as a college student. At first it was just a temp job reviewing copies of documents on microfiche, but she rose through the ranks, becoming the highest-ranking nonlawyer in the firm. "It's truly a place of opportunity—if you're hardworking and dedicated," she says.

Olivia Rubio, a freshman at Christ the King, appreciates the demanding but supportive environment at the law firm. "I don't feel scared to ask something," she says in a soft low voice. Olivia is petite, and her large glasses and Catholic school uniform—khaki skirt and a school sweater vest over a white-collared shirt—make her look younger than she is. She sits at a computer doing data entry in Central Support, a long white utilitarian room with copy machine after copy machine. Her supervisor, Wendy Tirado, praises her work ethic and care for detail. Tirado also joined the firm in an entry-level position and to her surprise was promoted to Central Support manager.

Around the corner from Central Support, Clara Santos works in a cubicle in the accounting department. As a graduate of Christ the King, she no longer wears a uniform, but a pink sundress and work-appropriate flats. Like Olivia, Clara worked in the mailroom as a student, moving to her current department for her senior year. As a senior about to head off to college, Clara was curious about what took place in the wood-paneled offices upstairs. Like any Gibbons employee could, Clara took advantage of her position, shadowing a sports lawyer and deciding that she would like to pursue law. She is majoring in biomedical engineering at St. Michael's College in Vermont and is looking into patent law. Away at school, she stayed in touch with her supervisors and applied for summer employment. Her relationships—and reputation for being a dependable worker— helped her secure a summer job.

Seeing Clara come back to her job site impressed Olivia. "When you work in places like this and do a good job, you can come back and get a job, and I think that's cool," she says. "Not many people can say, 'I worked at a law firm.'"

The graduates of Cristo Rey programs are better prepared for the working world than most college graduates or law students, Inderwies says. Though she has read none of the academic research on the importance of character traits, Inderwies understands it intuitively. "Academics alone is not the recipe for success in college," she says. "It's so frustrating to sit in an interview with someone who has been through high school, through college, they have this great degree, but they don't have one ounce of practical experience, and they have no idea what they want to do."

Down the street from Gibbons in downtown Newark, Horizon Blue Cross Blue Shield of New Jersey is another company that understands and implements the work-study program well, Inderwies says. As board chair, she often asks representatives from Horizon to come to new-sponsor events that bring potential clients, the school, and current clients together. Few companies can offer the kind of experience for students that Horizon can.

In the offices of many corporate sponsors, students work with few other people of color. Their training sessions in the summer prepare them to deal with being a minority in the workplace, making them aware of the perceptions that some may have of inner-city kids. But in Horizon's downtown Newark offices, the faces in the elevator reflect the diversity of Cristo Rey students. In her office with a distant view of the Manhattan skyline, Alison Banks-Moore is surrounded by awards celebrating Horizon's dedication to diversity.

As chief diversity officer, Banks-Moore leads a number of programs to help minority employees rise in the ranks as well as to prepare young people from minority communities to become future employees at Horizon. When Banks-Moore looks at the economic benefits of the Cristo Rey program, she does not think of the tasks students accomplish day to day, but what they might be able to do over the course of their careers. "We see it as teaching them," she says. "This is our future. If we're not going to do it, who's going to do it?"

Student workers at Horizon have assignments beyond what their corporate work-study department expects of them. Every month, students must write a reflection about what they have been working on and go over it with their supervisor. "I don't want them to just come in and do work and leave, because that's not what I do. I want it to stick," Banks-Moore says. "It's really important to understand why you're doing what you're doing."

She and work-study supervisor Xavia Mitchell, both African-American women, also try to provide a supportive environment for the teens. "We're mothers, sisters, and aunts in addition to work supervisors," Mitchell says. They often give advice to students—unsolicited, Banks-Moore adds with a laugh.

Christ the King senior James Mann says their advice is invaluable. "Sometimes it gets you through a week or month," he says. He also appreciates that Horizon connects students with mentors other than their supervisor, giving them another touch point at the organization. As a freshman James was connected with a mentor based on their shared love of basketball, and the two clicked. James can call him at home and even ask his wife, a high-school math teacher, for homework help. The two have gone to a New Jersey Nets game together, and they also attended a college convention. His mentor helped him decide to attend Montclair University. As an in-state school, it is a smart financial decision, James says. It is also diverse—a quality he has learned to value at Horizon. Mitchell also set James up to go to lunch with an accountant at Horizon, one of the career paths he is interested in. The accountant's praise of Montclair's business program clinched James's college decision.

Confident, talkative, and charming, James is an all-star worker at Horizon. Though Newark students generally move around to various jobs, Horizon requested to have James back all four years of his high-school career. The Human Resources department "stole him" from Physician Services, where he worked as a freshman. "That's what happens when you manage the program," Banks-Moore laughs. "You get to pick who you want."

James smiles as he remembers his first day of work as a freshman. He was invited to a meeting and "it sounded like a whole other language," he recalls. Then as a sophomore, he facilitated a meeting, introducing agenda items and speakers.

The HR department organizes a program for "Take Your Child to Work Day," which allows employees to expose their children to the working world and help them start thinking about careers. As a sophomore, James participated as if he were an employee's child, enjoying the organized activities and presentations. As a senior, James had more responsibilities. After the event, he put together a report on the program, compiling the results of a survey, so that the HR department could see which programs and activities the participants preferred.

Such a project may take him two or three drafts, but a little extra time is worth helping the students grow, Mitchell says. Because she knew that James is interested in accounting, Mitchell recently pulled him over to her computer while she worked on a project. She was creating pivot tables in Excel and knew that he would need to know how to create and use them as well. It might have taken her fifteen minutes to explain what she was doing; then she said, "Okay, let's switch seats. You sit in my chair, and you drive."

"He just got so excited because he was able to get this pivot table down," Mitchell says as James sat next to her, looking down in his lap bashfully but smiling. "It's not so much the work they're going to remember; it's the interaction with the people; it's the skills that they're going to be able to transfer into their college years," Mitchell adds.

Like Clara at Gibbons, James may be back at Horizon after his freshman year of college. Horizon is already recruiting him for INROADS, an internship program designed to give disadvantaged college students exposure to the corporate world. It is essentially the same as the Cristo Rey work program—only James would have even greater responsibilities, the paycheck would go directly to him, and he would be one step closer to securing a full-time job upon college graduation.

More Than a Job

The work-study program sometimes affects the company and its employees as much as the student worker. As an old friend of Father T. J. Martinez, Jeb Bashaw signed on to be one of the first corporate work sponsors for Cristo Rey Jesuit in Houston before it launched. When the school opened in 2009, though, the country was in the middle of a recession. It could not have been a worse time for James E. Bashaw & Company, a private wealth-management firm, to take on student workers. "This is the one time in my life I literally prayed to God. Usually I make secular decisions in my secular time," Bashaw says with a chuckle. He almost called Martinez four times to back out. Every time he was about to pick up the phone, something good would happen—the firm would get a new client or have a record day. "This is God telling me, quit being such a jackass and step it up," Bashaw says.

Still, Bashaw and his staff were skeptical about hiring fourteen-year-old students to work in the office. "I remember thinking, what in the world are we getting ourselves into? We're basically running a glorified romper room," he says.

David Lorenzo convinced the company otherwise. Even as a freshman, he was eager to contribute and be part of an organization, Bashaw says. Shy and a bit awkward, David nevertheless had a work ethic that impressed his supervisor, Laura Thompson, vice president of client services. She sent a letter to the school detailing his good work, and at the end of the school's first year he won a work-study award. Thompson attended the ceremony, where she met his mom and saw David come out of his shell. "He was just so excited about life, and it was a side we hadn't seen before," she says. "Each year he continued becoming more confident."

David was one of only three of the original class that stuck with their original employer all four years. David's loyalty—when he could have gone and chased a work-study placement at a big oil company—meant a lot to the family business. "When you have them for all four years, they can really grow and become part of the organization," Thompson says. "We just grew to love him. He became a part of our family."

Working with the student workers has made Thompson more patient and understanding in a work environment where it is often difficult to stop and take a breath, she says. It is a privilege to watch the kids grow and develop a sense of pride, Thompson adds. "When you tell them, 'Good job,' and they start beaming in front of you, there's nothing better than that. Cristo Rey is always thanking us for being sponsors, but I always wanted to thank them for letting us be a part of it."

The firm donates 2 percent of its top-line revenues annually to charity, Bashaw says, but having students from Cristo Rey in the office every day does more for the firm culture than donations. "It reinforces the idea that we're bigger than just taking care of rich people's money. We're giving back to the community in a way that is very personal," he says. Over twelve years, his firm grew from one man and a secretary managing $38 million to fifty employees in four cities managing $1 billion. "I had a lot of people help me along the way. Having these kids here reminds me, 'You know what, smarty pants, you're not as smart as you think you are, and you started somewhere.'"

Like David, Bashaw got his start with the Jesuits. His grandfather had been a tailor, and his father had been a sales manager, each generation doing better economically than the previous one. His father, however, passed away when Bashaw was just seven. When he got to high school, his mother could not afford the $1,500 tuition to send him to Strake Jesuit College Preparatory, but the Jesuits gave him a $500 scholarship. His mom paid another $500, and Bashaw made up the final $500 by working at the school every summer for $1 an hour.

"I think about what would have happened thirty-six years ago if the Jesuits hadn't taken a chance on me," he says. Thanks to his business success, Bashaw was able to pay full tuition for his son at Strake Jesuit. Signing a check for $14,000 for his son's freshman year filled him with happiness. David, also the son of a single mother, deserved the same chance he had to achieve success with a Jesuit education, Bashaw thought.

By the end of his senior year, David had chosen to attend University of Houston, Bashaw's alma mater. He was attracted to its business and engineering programs, and it also would be cheaper to go to school locally. He still was not sure how he was going to pay tuition.

On his last day of work his senior year, David and Bashaw happened to get into the elevator at the same time. Bashaw asked if he was going to live on campus, and David said, "I don't think I can do that. There's just not enough money," Bashaw recalls.

Many work-study sponsors give their students gifts upon graduation—money, a college gift basket, or even a computer—so David was not surprised that the company had planned a farewell luncheon in his honor. During the luncheon, Bashaw came over to him. "Out of nowhere he starts giving this wonderful speech about me being at the company," David says. David was flattered, but did not think much of it—until Bashaw announced his gift: he was giving David a full-ride scholarship to college, including room and board.

David was in shock. "I thought it was a dream," he says. He gave Bashaw a hug and, with his voice stuttering, the once shy David gave his own speech, thanking Bashaw and Thompson not only for the scholarship, but also for the four years of experience.

"There wasn't a dry eye in the room," Thompson recalls. "It was like Jeb was sending one of his children off to school."

Bashaw, in fact, looked over at his daughter, who graduated from the University of Notre Dame in 2012, to steady himself during the luncheon ceremony. Funding David's college education had been a family decision. As a corporate sponsor, Bashaw has been able to remind his family, his company, and himself of the values he holds dear. "It's not just about us having the biggest bank account," he says. "Everything we have here is on loan from God."

CHAPTER SIX

Faith and Grit

A few days before David and his classmates became the first graduates of Cristo Rey Jesuit College Preparatory School in Houston, they gathered at school for a final day of retreat. While the underclassmen took finals, still dressed in uniforms, the seniors were dressed in jeans and T-shirts, many emblazoned with Cristo Rey logos.

Andrew Hoyt, who had served as their English teacher for three and a half years before his wife's job required that he move away from Houston, had returned for graduation week to lead the senior retreat.

Back in the first days of Cristo Rey Jesuit, Hoyt had given his then freshmen a pep talk—he was excited that they would graduate and go on to college. Veronica Flores called him out. "You don't really care if we graduate," he remembers her saying, rolling her eyes. "You just want to drown us in homework."

"It was half funny and half Veronica saying, 'I don't think you really care,'" Hoyt recalls. He responded with a promise: if she graduated from high school and got into college, he would fill up a classroom with homework and let her swim in it.

Veronica did not lack for ambition. As a freshman, she already had her eye on college, wanting to work in the medical field. She had two supportive parents, both working hard in low-wage jobs to put their daughter through Catholic elementary school. But she also had a bit of an attitude.

"She has a perfect radar for anything that's saccharine, too enthusiastic, hackneyed," Hoyt adds—including an excited teacher or an over-the-top school president like Father T. J. Martinez, SJ.

Veronica admits that she did not like Cristo Rey Jesuit or its energetic leader at first. "Father Martinez was always happy, and I was like, 'Ugh, why are you so loud?'" she laughs.

But as she sat in the first all-school Mass with her classmates, her attitude started to soften. Instead of thinking of high school as just a stepping-stone to college, she started seeing her classmates as a community. Retreat after retreat solidified the feeling, and by the time she was a senior, Veronica found herself applying to Jesuit universities so that she could find a similar spiritual community in college. She celebrated with Martinez, the always happy, loud Jesuit school president, when she became the first student to be accepted at a Jesuit university. She ultimately chose to go to Regis University, a Jesuit school in Denver.

Despite moving away, Hoyt had not forgotten his promise to Veronica and her classmates to be there for their graduation. He planned the senior retreat as a day "off" in the midst of a week full of ceremonies and cameras. Even as teachers and administrators went about their end-of-the-year duties collecting and organizing textbooks and steaming graduation gowns, the seniors fell easily into reflective retreat mode at the school. They paired off, walking around the basketball court and lying on the bleachers, and talked about the people for whom they were grateful. Over the previous four years, the school had become a place where they could let down their guard. "These kids trust that we have something in store for them, that there's some depth of experience that they can access here," Hoyt says.

But Hoyt also scheduled some fun into the retreat. Before they started their day of reflection, Veronica was sent to the college counseling office. There, Hoyt and her classmates were waiting, having filled part of the room with a year's worth of crumpled homework at least a meter high. Veronica jumped in and swam. Even though she had long given up her cynical side, the little prank was symbolic, Hoyt says. "It speaks to the depth, strength, and longevity of the relationships you form in this school."

It is not enough to earn good grades as a Cristo Rey student; the high expectations of the schools extend to students' character as well. Cristo Rey schools foster an environment where students can grow academically, professionally, and personally. The focus on character development is rooted in the Catholic faith, but it also reflects the latest research on the qualities that lead to success.

What It Means to Be a Catholic School

If the goal is to go to college, any number of good public, charter, or private schools can get students there, says Cristo Rey Boston admissions director Marcos Enrique. At a Cristo Rey school, they also will have to attend Masses and retreats. Their teachers will lead prayers during science class, and they will learn about the Bible and other religions in four years of religious studies classes. Crosses and religious artwork will surround them in hallways and classrooms. Cristo Rey schools are unmistakably Catholic, and they want their students to faithfully follow the teachings of Jesus—or, if they are not Christian, to respect them. Still, a Cristo Rey school is Catholic not only in its outward symbols, but also in its vision of education, Enrique says.

"One danger in schools is to narrow down education to learning and learning ultimately to training," Enrique says. If you ask students why they want to go to a good high school and then to college, they say it is to get a good job. It is a mentality that says, "If I have what I don't have now, then I will be happy," he says. But the problem with always trying to get to a better life is that there is always something better, he adds. Whether in school or at work, "You are as good as what you can accomplish."

Cristo Rey schools have to help students set their sights high—ready to rise out of poverty and succeed in corporate America—while also helping them understand that their goals should be about more than making money. This has always been a balancing act for Catholic schools, according to *Catholic Schools and the Common Good:* "While schools are committed to preparing students with the intellectual and social competencies required for functioning in contemporary middle-class American life, they also seek to hone a critical consciousness toward social life as it should be. Students are to be competent in modern society, but never totally at ease."[1]

These big ideas are far from the minds of a small group of restless sophomores at Cristo Rey Boston who say they have hit the "sophomore slump." They complain about the dress code, long hours, hard work, and lack of electives. Teachers and classmates are supportive, they say, and if you are willing to work, the school will get you ready for college. But the program forces them to grow up quickly. "It's great. I just wish I could be a teenager," one girl says.

Young students sometimes complain that they cannot "be themselves" at Cristo Rey schools, but Enrique counters that the Cristo Rey program aims to help students find their true selves—to understand their internal worth and bring their gifts to the community. "The mission of education is to propose to students that, in and of themselves, they have a value," Enrique says. All teenagers are in the process of finding their worth, but "in the inner city, where a lot of families are coming—for a lack of a better word—from hell, there's a serious need for a place where students can go to receive that."

From this perspective, college success is not the goal, but the product of a Cristo Rey school, Enrique says. It is a measurable outcome of how well Cristo Rey schools convince their students of their own worth. "If they are able to love themselves, then they will love what they do, and then they'll go to college," he says. "We are not interested in student achievement for its own sake."

Finding one's internal worth is about more than self-esteem; it is rooted in the idea that each human person has dignity as a child of God. This foundational idea of Catholic social thought, in turn, drives *cura personalis,* the care for the entire person through education. The "graduate at graduation," as the schools call their model student, is open to growth, spiritual, intellectually motivated, loving, work experienced, and committed to doing justice.

Even though not all students are Catholic, let alone Christian, character development is for everyone. By cultivating these intrinsic qualities, Cristo Rey schools prepare students to deal with challenges on their path. This is what differentiates Catholic schools from the military or strict charter schools that impose discipline by enforcement. Their organizational beliefs, notes *Catholic Schools and the Common Good,* are "expansive, liberating, and humanizing rather than narrow, restrictive, and closed."[2]

GRIT: CAN CHARACTER BE TAUGHT?

Generations of Catholic-school graduates credit the firm but loving discipline of Catholic nuns for their success. In recent years, the academic world has substantiated the benefits of long-standing Catholic values with research that shows the importance of attitude and behavior. Although Cristo Rey schools are grounded in faith, they do not limit their personal development programs to the Catholic tradition; they also learn from the secular education world's discussion of character.

Perhaps the most widely discussed character trait in the education world today is *grit,* or persistence. University of Pennsylvania psychologist Angela Lee Duckworth defines grit as the "tendency to sustain interest in and effort toward very long-term goals."[3] Her inspiration for this definition comes from Mattie Ross, the fourteen-year-old character in *True Grit,* a novel that has been made into two movies. "It's really about this young girl who against all odds pursues a very long-term, almost impossible goal and eventually, eventually—with an emphasis on 'eventually'— succeeds in that goal," she explains in a 2009 *TEDx* talk.[4] "It's the stamina quality—not just being passionate, but sustaining that over a long time."

As a seventh-grade math teacher, Duckworth found that her students who were the smartest according to their IQ scores were not always the ones who did the best in her class.[5] Curious about what made people successful, she enrolled in graduate school to study psychology. Since then, Duckworth has conducted studies in a variety of settings, from West Point Academy to the National Spelling Bee. More than measures of talent, she found that grit and self-control are the best predictors of success in all of the settings.

Cristo Rey schools often teach their students about academic ideas like grit. In Cristo Rey Boston advisory periods, for instance, students take Duckworth's self-assessment test that measures their level of "grittiness." They also read stories of people like Walt Disney and discuss what about these successful figures helped them persevere through challenges to achieve their dreams. Everyone can increase their level of grittiness, advisers tell their students.

Most of us think of character as "something innate and unchanging," Paul Tough writes in *How Children Succeed: Grit, Curiosity, and the Hidden Power of Character*, his bestselling book summarizing much of the academic research on character and education. Researchers, however, see it differently. They define character as malleable abilities. "They are skills you can learn; they are skills you can practice; and they are skills you can teach," Tough writes.[6]

As with all Catholic schools, some could argue that Cristo Rey schools are selective. Although most students enter two years below grade level, they often have fewer disciplinary issues and absences in middle school. Even if Cristo Rey schools do not seek out academic superstars, some wonder if they choose the students with strong character, those who already have the grit to graduate from any high school and go on to college. The question is whether Cristo Rey students succeed because they enter with grit or whether the schools can help students develop it.

On the one hand, good students with grit deserve the best preparation for college that they can afford—which may be a Cristo Rey school. And the rigorous program does not work for everyone. On average, schools retained only 57 percent of students from ninth grade to graduation for the class of 2013 (the average hides great variations from school to school). Part of the challenge is that Cristo Rey schools serve an often highly mobile low-income population. Unpredictable factors such as a parent's deportation or employment opportunities or the availability of affordable housing affect student retention. More than 40 percent of students who withdrew from a Cristo Rey Network school in the 2012–13 school year did so for reasons out of the school's control. Another

32 percent of students who leave the school, though, do so because they could not keep up academically. The schools also expel students who flagrantly violate rules or are fired from work twice, accounting for 15 and 4 percent of withdrawals and dismissals, respectively.[7]

On the other hand, Cristo Rey educators believe that their model can work for all students, and they are dedicated to improving their schools' retention numbers. Buoyed by a faith in the dignity of all persons, they believe that all children have the grit and character to succeed within them; they just need help finding it. And if the schools can help students find that grit within themselves, they think the number of dismissals due to disciplinary and academic reasons will fall. Although the numbers do not yet match their ideal, they know, anecdotally at least, that it is possible to teach their students character skills like grit.

"It's like a lock you're trying to open to get them to understand that they can achieve, they can be successful," says Father Gregory Gebbia, principal of Christ the King Preparatory School in Newark. You just need to find the right combination. The first key, though, comes from a student's home.

The Starting Point

Jasmine Young is one of the students who should not have succeeded. She is the oldest of four, raised by her grandmother in a neighborhood not far from Cristo Rey Jesuit in Houston. Her mother is not in the picture; she is in and out of rehab. Even when she is clean, Jasmine's grandmother Regina Bray explains, their neighborhood is full of drug dealers—not a healthy environment for an addict. The last time Jasmine's grandmother talked to her daughter, the daughter told the mother that she did not want to come home for fear of disappointing her.

Although it is hard for Bray to see her daughter suffer, it is also hard for a grandmother to raise a second set of children in a home not big enough for five. She used to give Jasmine her bedroom to study and sleep, but Jasmine moved to the couch in the den when Bray had a heart attack. Bray is thin like her granddaughter and looks healthy, but the stress of her life had gotten to her. She is divorced and works as a seamstress. When Jasmine applied for Cristo Rey, Bray wrote that she could afford to pay just $25 a month for tuition. But it is not just finances that bring her stress. "I cannot be a grandmother," she says. "I'm Mommy and Daddy. I'm saddened because I cannot be grandmother, because grandmothers are supposed to be all sweet."

As they get older, Bray says, her grandchildren sometimes become angry—that their mom is not there for them, that their grandmother has to discipline rather than spoil them. Jasmine keeps her anger inside, but Bray can see it.

Perseverance, Duckworth writes, comes from both nurture and nature.[8] Environmental factors can influence a child's success in school and beyond. The research shows that this is both a positive and a negative for students like Jasmine. Her home life and parenting from the day she was born have a huge impact on her life outcomes, but interventions through adolescence can counter early influences.

On the negative side, many of our life results can be traced back to Adverse Childhood Experiences (ACE). A high ACE score—meaning a high incidence of household dysfunction, neglect, or abuse, for instance—is strongly correlated with negative health outcomes, regardless of behavior.[9] The culprit is stress, explains Tough. The way our body deals with stress causes wear and tear, and too much stress in a person's infancy and childhood can cause long-lasting physical, psychological, and neurological effects. "If the body's stress-management systems are overworked, they eventually break down under the strain," Tough writes, summarizing the research of Bruce McEwen, a neuroendocrinologist at Rockefeller University.[10]

The effect of stress can be mitigated by good parenting, though. Michael Meeney, a neuroscientist at McGill University, first found an interesting pattern in rats. Pups that had been licked and groomed a great deal by their mothers had much better life outcomes down the line. They were better at mazes, more social, and lived longer.[11] Other researchers followed up on his observations and found evidence of a similar pattern in humans. When mothers are responsive to their babies, children form a "secure attachment." These children handle stress better than those whose mothers were not responsive, even when the child experiences environmental risks like family turmoil. "High-quality mothering, in other words, can act as a powerful buffer against the damage that adversity inflicts on a child's stress-response system, much as the dams' licking and grooming seemed to protect their pups," Tough summarizes.[12]

The ability to deal with stress has a huge impact on a child's education. Following children through high school, one group of researchers found that the responsiveness of a parent early in life predicted which children would graduate more reliably than IQ or achievement-test scores.[13] In the developing brain, the prefrontal cortex is particularly vulnerable to stress, and this part of the brain regulates emotions and thoughts. Growing up in a stressful environment compromises a student's ability to concentrate, follow directions, and rebound from disappointment. Stress also hurts students' executive function—"the ability to deal with confusing and unpredictable situations and information."[14] Unsurprisingly, researchers have found a strong correlation between high ACE scores and problems in school.[15]

It is unknown how Jasmine and her siblings were parented in the first years of their lives, but the struggles of countless Cristo Rey students are understandable—predictable even—when research into the effects of stress are considered. Many students are raised by parents or guardians who struggle to stay employed, who had children when they were teenagers themselves, or who are addicted to drugs or alcohol. Though students must have legal immigration status to participate in the corporate work-study program, their parents might be undocumented. The threat of deportation can be a constant stress in a family's life. Grandmothers like Bray are firm but loving, selflessly giving their grandchildren the best opportunities they can when they should be approaching retirement, but grandmotherly love cannot make up for the pain of being abandoned by parents.

Many students also come from families with two hardworking parents—perhaps working multiple jobs to make ends meet.

But even in the most stable of families, Cristo Rey students live in neighborhoods where they see gang violence, drug use, and teen pregnancy regularly. As Andy Laureano, associate director of college initiatives at the Cristo Rey Network and a 2006 graduate of Cristo Rey Jesuit in Chicago, puts it, simply not becoming a parent by sixteen is a success in the neighborhood he grew up in. "It's not to say that my parents didn't support me, but they just had a skewed version of what success was," Laureano says.

It is difficult, psychologist Alicia Lieberman explains to Tough, for even the best parents to be responsive to their children in such environments. "When you are bombarded by poverty, uncertainty, and fear, it takes a superhuman quality to provide the conditions for a secure attachment," she says.[16]

The good news for Cristo Rey students is that, despite being vulnerable to stress, the prefrontal cortex is also responsive to intervention during adolescence and early adulthood.[17] Interventions that work mitigate the stressors and help young people deal with the stress when it is unavoidable. To do so, Cristo Rey schools try to supplement—though not replace—students' families by creating a loving, supportive environment.

Jasmine is mild-mannered and quiet. Bray feared sending her to one of the local public high schools. A devout Catholic, Bray prayed about what to do and soon after received a postcard advertising an open house for Cristo Rey Jesuit. The school was still under renovation when she visited, but watching a video about the Network, she knew she had found the answer to her prayers. The students in the video exuded a positive spirit, she says. Jasmine agreed to attend Cristo Rey Jesuit without protest or enthusiasm.

In her first two years at the school, Jasmine struggled academically. Hoyt remembers that she would turn in assignments late or incomplete for his English classes. But at the end of her sophomore year, she turned in a couple of reflections about her own life, and he was impressed with her writing. "I started to stoke that," Hoyt says. "You have a real writer inside you. We've got to work this out," he told her.

After that, he saw Jasmine come to life. It was not just uncovering a talent. "It was uncovering something she likes to work on, that she can get better at," Hoyt says. Jasmine found the resilience to work on her writing, even when it was hard and when everything else around her was chaotic at best, he adds.

It was around that time that college first crossed her mind, Jasmine says. "I didn't believe in myself. I didn't know how to believe in myself," she says. "They taught us to believe in ourselves at all times and that there's no such thing as impossible."

The academic program challenged Jasmine. "It's overwhelming and really hard to the point where you might give up," Jasmine says. "But the people here tell you, 'Don't give up, don't give up,' pushing you and pushing you until you're succeeding."

Jasmine, though, needed more than encouraging teachers. She made use of the counselors at the school and liked that she could talk openly about her life with teachers and friends. Jasmine is not Catholic, but she appreciated the religious side of the school and is considering joining the church. Cristo Rey helped her grow closer to God, she says. At Masses and retreats, she learned that she cannot do everything alone; she needs God's support. Jasmine attributes her grandmother's healing after her heart attack to prayer.

Though she got into a design school in California—her first passion is fashion—Jasmine decided to attend University of Houston instead. Jasmine says that she will continue drawing while majoring in business. She hopes to own her own design business someday. Bray worries that living at home will hold her back, but Jasmine wants to stay close to her family. She wants to be able to help her grandmother raise her younger siblings.

Jasmine's next youngest sibling, Jada, should be in high school. Though the two are close in age, Jada could not be convinced to attend Cristo Rey Jesuit. After going to the same public high school that Jasmine was supposed to attend, Jada dropped out. Jasmine and Jada also have two younger brothers in elementary school. They want to go to Cristo Rey, Jasmine says, but she wants to be there to make sure they follow in her footsteps. Jasmine is sure that, had she gone to Jada's school, she too would have dropped out. Nobody told Jada what you can do if you complete school, Jasmine says. "I think if she came to my high school, she probably would have been just like me, and she would still be in school."

A School Family

At the end of their senior retreat, Jasmine and her classmates changed from their jeans and T-shirts to their Sunday best in preparation for their Baccalaureate Mass at the Co-Cathedral of Sacred Heart. They buzzed around an archdiocesan meeting room, straightening hair, adjusting ties, and taking pictures with

each other. On a patio overlooking the cathedral, Jasmine stood
tall above her friends, posing in a sleek striped dress accented by a
belt, fitting for her career interest.

Before distributing their black gowns and yellow capes, David
Garcia-Pratz, dean of academics, asked for their attention. He
just wanted to say "I love you" to the group one last time, he said.
A scene that might have seemed strange in any other school was
natural and heartfelt in a Cristo Rey community. "Cristo Rey
Jesuit is a family," Jasmine explains.

The *Catholic Schools and the Common Good* researchers heard
that a lot when they visited Catholic schools—so often, in fact,
that they decided to measure the level of community and its
impact at the schools. They found that the claim of community is
not just a platitude, but an "organizational reality" that character-
izes Catholic schools.[18] Based on measurements of shared values,
shared activities, and social relations, Catholic schools are, in fact,
more "communal" than public schools.

Being communal proved to be an effective educational strategy. Their analysis found that a sense of community was largely
responsible for teachers' enjoyment of their work and staff morale,
and somewhat responsible for teacher efficacy. It also had a pro-
found, though slightly smaller impact on student outcomes, de-
creasing the prevalence of class cutting, classroom disorder, and
dropping out, and increasing interest in academics.[19] The sense of
community at Catholic schools stood in sharp contrast to the educational bureaucracies of public schools. Educational bureaucracy
created "student passivity and teacher alienation," the researchers
wrote. "A reliance on specialization and centralization has pro-

moted a breakdown in human commitment and contributed to the creation of transient relationships, a disintegration of common bonds, and a retreat from shared responsibility."[20]

All Cristo Rey schools create a culture that promotes shared responsibility in different ways, but one key part of the Cristo Rey family is that it seeks to include, not displace, a student's family at home. At the very minimum, parents need to "buy in" to the program by agreeing to pay tuition. Although the work-study program and scholarships pay most of the tuition, paying even $25 a month gives parents a greater commitment to the program.

Schools also must earn parents' trust, a difficult proposition in communities where trust is often broken. "They see in us a willingness and a sincere desire to help them, not just to be a place where they send their kids, but to help their family," Enrique, the Cristo Rey Boston admissions director, says. "Once you build that trust, then you become a reference point for everything." Parents come to him not only about admissions, but also about classes, church, and jobs.

Elizabeth Ortiz completely trusts Cristo Rey Boston. After her son graduated from North Cambridge Catholic in 2010 (it was already a Cristo Rey–model school), she kept returning to the school for help filling out his financial-aid papers for college. She also enrolled her younger daughter in the school. Ortiz is the type of parent who introduces herself to teachers at the beginning of the school year. "I prefer you to call me when there's a problem instead of calling me when my son is failing the class and there's nothing we can do then," she tells them. She expects As and Bs and takes away TV privileges if her children do not meet those expectations. Like all Cristo Rey schools, Cristo Rey Boston has an online system on which parents can see grades and comments from teachers. Parents and teachers maintain open communication through e-mail as well. The school often hosts events in the evening, so parents do not have to miss work to participate. Ortiz likes to see that many other parents also are involved with their children's education, showing up to open houses, report-card nights, and conferences in greater numbers than they would at public schools.

After her son graduated from high school, Ortiz was laid off from a company where she had worked for fifteen years. She had been out of work for a year when she visited the school for help with financial-aid forms. There she found out that Cristo Rey Boston was looking for a front-desk manager. Cristo Rey schools often tap their local communities for employees. Doing so, in fact, is a requirement of the third Mission Effectiveness Standard: "A Cristo Rey school is family centered and plays an active role in the local community." As a bilingual receptionist who knew and loved the school, Ortiz was an ideal candidate.

Now as the front-desk manager, Ortiz is the school's first line of response when parents call in. Not all parents understand themselves as working as a team with the school, she says. Whether it is a confiscated cell phone or a bad grade, parents may side with their child over the school if they have not found the trust that Enrique describes.

Sometimes parents call in upset that their student is not doing well. "If the students need help and support, teachers are here until 7:00 o'clock at night," Ortiz tells them. She is often the one telling the teachers to go home, she notes. Just as she does for her own children, she advises them to log on to the online reporting system to see teachers' comments and to listen to their point of view.

One parent called saying she did not know what to do to get her son to school on time. Ortiz guessed correctly that he was sleeping in because he was up all night with his electronics. She suggested that the frustrated mom take away his electronics for every day that he is late to school. When parents say, "You don't understand," Ortiz says, it helps that she can tell them, "I'm a parent myself, so I know what you're going through."

Cristo Rey Boston is reaching out to parents as well. It has a family engagement team, and a volunteer speaks with the parents of a small group of freshmen at least once a week. The school has instituted a policy of reaching out to parents when their students do things well, instead of only when they are in trouble or struggling.

In Los Angeles, Verbum Dei High School tries to develop a personal, trusting relationship with parents by requiring a thirty-hour annual service commitment. Parents can fulfill their hours by supplying food for events or paying $10 per hour, but the school prefers that parents volunteer at the school, so that they can get to know teachers and staff on a personal level. When students see their history teacher or work-study coordinator talking with their moms before school, they know that whatever they do at school or work will not escape their parents.

Verbum Dei's parental involvement is not all work, though. On a Saturday morning in May, many of the Verbum Dei boys have brought their mothers and grandmothers to school for a Mother's Day brunch. The multipurpose room, usually set up as a theater, has been transformed into a restaurant. While teachers and volunteers cook eggs in the kitchen, sons and their mothers, grandmothers, aunts, and a few other family members—about 150 people total—sit around fifteen large round tables covered by yellow tablecloths. As they nibble on Mexican pastries and muffins, Edin Barrera, a Jesuit novice, leads a presentation that includes a quiz on the Bible and a prayer. During a guided meditation, he asks the group to imagine their mothers. "You realize that your mother has been the face of God to you," he says in a smooth, calming voice with soft instrumental music in the background. "You know God, you know God's love for you, because of your mother's love for you."

Some of the younger boys cannot help opening their eyes during the meditation, peeking to see that their peers also have their eyes closed. Most, though, sit silently with bowed heads. Junior Jacob Palma holds hands with his grandmother.

After a blessing, Barrera gives them a chance to share a reflection or thank their mothers. After a few boys volunteer, many hands shoot up, as the boys ask to publicly declare their affection for their moms. Jacob takes the microphone and stands up to tell the room how much he appreciates his two maternal figures in spontaneous, heartfelt remarks: "My grandma and my mom— they're really amazing. They work every day. They have breakfast for me in the mornings. My mom comes from work, picks us up, even though she doesn't really want to. She wants to go to sleep. She has dinner ready for us. My grandmother is amazing.

She's there helping my mom, making sure we're doing okay. They sacrifice their weekends for me so that I can get my stuff done. They're there when I need them. They're really special to me. I don't know what I would do without them, and I want to thank them."

Most of the boys' messages are similar, but each one garners "awws" and applause. Mothers tear up or laugh at their sons' jokes. Like Jacob, the boys lean down to hug their moms. The school holds a father-son event too, but many of the boys are raised by single mothers and grandmothers. Jacob and his younger brother Alexander, a sophomore, both say that their mother is the one pushing them along. When Jacob did not want to go to school one day, his mom said, "Okay, then go sort through the trash cans and see what you find." That is what he would end up doing if he did not go to school, laughs his mother, Rosalie Palma, recalling the morning. "If we didn't go to college, my mom would be really disappointed," Jacob says.[21]

From the beginning, the school made it clear to Rosalie that it is not an elevator, where you're just going to come the fourth year and see your son graduate, Palma says. During the admissions interviews, she was asked questions: What was her son's favorite subject? What would she do if the school called her because her son got in trouble? How would she react? Would she be willing to come to the school and help out?

Although the school demands a lot of parents, the family-like atmosphere is not just for her sons; Palma feels a part of it too. By the second week of school, teachers and the dean greeted her by name when she was on campus. She was surprised and impressed. She remembers feeling lost at an open house for another Catholic high school that was too big to feel like home. "It's not that they don't care at the other schools, but here they're on top of everything," Palma says.

ESTABLISHING DISCIPLINE

Just as Alexander and Jacob have their mother's pushing and Jasmine has her grandmother's support, Cristo Rey students who do the best despite all obstacles have at least one supportive figure in their lives outside of the school, says Father Robert Sandoz, the president of Christ the King in Newark. It does not need to be a parent, and the support this person needs to provide is not major. Students simply need somebody who is stable—a grandparent, an older sibling—checking to see if they are doing their homework, going to bed on time, and eating breakfast. "The person we're looking for at home is really the support for students to follow through on what they *know* they need to do," Sandoz says. Still children, high-school students legitimately need help at home, he explains. The school is also there, though, to help instill in them an internal sense of discipline that will help them be successful.

Sandoz and his fellow Franciscan Father Gregory Gebbia, who served as dean of students before becoming principal in 2013, helped build a culture of discipline at Christ the King. The two priests wear black clerics to work every day, but often leave their Román collars flapping free. Sandoz's calm, gentle personality complements Gebbia's animated personality. When the two drive into Manhattan for an event, Gebbia takes the wheel, aggressively winding them through traffic, while Sandoz prays in the passenger seat. Gebbia has an enthusiasm for life that is evident whether driving, laughing, or eating—food is one of a priest's pleasures, he jokes. But when Gebbia's friendly mustached face turns stern, he can strike fear in Christ the King students. Gebbia employs both the qualities of a fun-loving uncle and strict disciplinarian as part of the combination to unlock students' potential.

When Sandoz and Gebbia arrived at the school, though, rules were not being enforced consistently. The school had limited resources and was struggling to stay afloat in its first few years, having launched just as the 2008 recession began. The physical environment—an old preschool with drab colors and tape all over— was less than inspiring, and students felt they had the liberty to use cell phones and talk back to adults. Small infractions gave way to a few more significant incidents: a boy threw a desk at a teacher; another lit a fire in the bathroom; a purse had been stolen.

Gebbia and Sandoz brought an all-out Franciscan assault on the school. "It was sort of blitzkrieg discipline," Gebbia says. "The students are going to hate my guts, but by Christmas you'll see a change in the culture of the school. And it will be clear why I'm doing it."

Gebbia's zero-tolerance approach helped nip violent and egregious behavior in the bud. Catholic schools' ability to provide a safe space for learning is a key element of their effectiveness in inner-city neighborhoods. Violence would be met with expulsion, no exceptions.

But even smaller issues of disrespect were met with strong consequences. Early on in his tenure, a girl came to school with six earrings instead of the allowed one per ear. Gebbia asked her multiple times to remove the earrings, and each time she ignored him. Finally, he threatened expulsion. Still, she simply walked away, ignoring him again. Gebbia had to escort her out of the building, and she was not welcome back.

The school's physical environment, Gebbia says, is as critical as enforcing the rules. As trained liturgists, both Sandoz and Gebbia pay close attention to how externals influence the internal spiritual life. Prayer services and Masses are planned to include the student body's many cultures, with prayers in Spanish and Creole music. Despite a tight academic schedule, art and music classes are valued, and Franciscan and culturally appropriate art decorate the otherwise sterile green brick hallway walls. Liturgy, art, and the physical environment are all part of the Franciscan conception of *cura personalis,* the education of the whole person.

During summer vacations, Gebbia has led volunteers in clean-ups of the classrooms. Employees and about a dozen students volunteered every day to make the school a more welcoming environment. Students donned rubber gloves to clean the tape off the walls, then painted the rooms in warm, bold colors. They loaded heavy, old wooden desks from the classrooms into a moving truck, unloaded them at a dump, and then picked up newer desks from an elite girls' prep school that was updating its furniture. All the tables, library shelves and books, study carrels, and office furniture were donated and moved in by volunteers. "If we had to purchase all these materials and furniture for these students, we would not be there for another five years," says Lisa Papciak, assistant director of development. "Environment is subliminal, but if you don't have a good environment, you'll see the results very quickly."

Each school day begins with the students' recitation of a prayer, the Pledge of Allegiance, and the school's mission statement. Though the mission statement is printed on the inside front cover of the student handbook, most students quickly memorize and internalize it. The handbook includes fifty pages of information about school culture and expectations, rules, and resources. Students and parents must sign it to acknowledge that they have read it.

Students like the safety of the school. "They like that nobody's going to hit them and get away with it here," Gebbia says. The fact that students voluntarily stay for Homework Center or hang out in the hallways after school—teachers have to tell them to go home eventually—is a testament to the culture the school has built. Sandoz recalls a time when more students than expected showed up for a Saturday detention. He pulled the students who were not supposed to be there out of the room and asked why they were there. "We'd rather be here on detention than in our house," Sandoz says they told him.

On Thursdays, the school stays open late for SCAN, or School Community Activity Night. The majority of the school stays until 7:00 or 8:00 P.M. to play board games in the classrooms or basketball in the gym. The night ends with prayer and pizza or sometimes a home-cooked meal prepared by Gebbia.

Newark's students enjoy SCAN, but, like Boston's sophomores, some underclassmen complain about having to be Christ the King students "365 days a year, 24/7." "Because we have to represent the school, we kind of lose our ability to be ourselves," says sophomore Emilia Glass.

She and a few classmates do not understand some of the rules, especially the dress code policies not allowing them to dye their hair or grow facial hair. You can look professional for work with facial hair, and it is not a gang symbol, they argue. Joseph Dillard, a hardworking student who goes to Homework Center voluntarily, says gangs only recruit kids who look as though they do not have a future. "If they see someone walking down the street, clean shaven . . . ," he says, then pauses, catching himself as he confirms the school's argument against facial hair.

The adults in Cristo Rey schools know how easy it is for even the best kids to wind up in a bad situation in inner-city neighborhoods. In 2003, Cristo Rey Chicago student Sergio Garcia was going home from a party with friends in the wee hours of a Sunday morning when another car pulled up and shot into the car, killing the promising junior. Sergio was not part of a gang and had recently earned the top PSAT score at Cristo Rey Chicago.

If being "yourself" as a teenager means going to parties and acting irresponsibly, Gebbia agrees that students cannot be themselves. At the beginning of the year, though, he offers a different identity. Gebbia tells students to look in the mirror twice a day and say, "I am a woman or man of promise."

The vast majority of Christ the King students—and Cristo Rey students in general—are good kids. They want to be women and men of promise. They do not get in trouble for fighting, but for chewing gum or wearing white socks. Detentions for seemingly little things are important, Gebbia says, helping students understand the expectations of the working world. Following Franciscan tradition, discipline is "formative, not punitive," he explains. "The rules here are to help a community of believers to be the Body of Christ—a body that functions together. I say, 'Excuse me,' not because of some strict moral code, but as an act of respect to you."

Gebbia also provides an out for students before they misbehave. If they feel as though they are going to snap at a teacher or a fellow student, all they have to do is ask to be dismissed to Father Greg's office, and teachers will let them leave class. At least once a week, a student will take advantage of this release valve, but it is not just a free pass. In Gebbia's office, they will sit at the corner of a large conference table donated to the school, and Gebbia will try to root out what is really going on.

Students may be on edge because they did not sleep the night before. They may be hungry because there is not enough food at home. When their teacher demands that they read something out loud, their minds may be someplace else, and they cannot. Maybe classmates are teasing a student who is dealing with an alcoholic or emotionally abusive parent at home. If the parent yelled at the student or said terrible things the night before, the student may feel like hitting the classmate. "It's really not about smacking that person; it's 'My dad isn't there for me. I'm raw, I'm sensitive,'" Gebbia explains. His discussions with students are about naming those feelings, he says.

A Catholic Charities counselor comes in four days a week, but she has a caseload and appointments. Gebbia offers an immediate response with a pastoral, rather than clinical approach. He may refer students to meet with the counselor, and he is mandated to report if students share stories of abuse. Students, though, think of his office as a safe space.

Because Gebbia is a priest and an educator, his approach to discipline is grounded in his own Franciscan formation, but it also aligns with psychology. Though he is not a therapist, Gebbia is essentially doing cognitive behavioral therapy with students. As Tough notes, teachers can even do this in the classroom. This type of therapy, he explains, "involves using the conscious mind to recognize negative or self-destructive thoughts or interpretations and to (sometimes literally) talk yourself into a better perspective."[22]

"Character formation," as Gebbia explains, "includes learning to reflect, because if you can't reflect, you can't see what you've done and then set new goals for where you want to be." When students come to his office, he does more than just allow them to vent about their frustrations at home. "If your dad isn't going to be there for you, how are you going to deal with this? How are you going to deal with this in a productive way, a meaningful way rather than a harmful or self-destructive way?" he will ask. "I always tell them, 'You're either getting bitter or better.'"

Gebbia is asking students to develop their metacognitive skills—thinking about thinking. Skills such as adaptability, initiative, self-control, and self-efficacy benefit not only students' personal development, but also their academic development. Paying as much attention to metacognition as content knowledge, college-readiness expert David Conley posits, could be "the missing link needed to close the achievement gap more rapidly and effectively."[23]

At Cristo Rey schools, it is hard to separate discipline, personal and spiritual development, academic growth, and work performance. The "open to growth" mind-set celebrated in the "graduate at graduation" qualities touches on all of these areas. At the work program's boot camp, religious retreats, and advisory periods, teachers and staff talk with students about the mind-set and skills that researchers have shown will help them find success. Terms like "grit" provide a common language for Cristo Rey students across the country. In the classroom, and increasingly at their work sites, colorful APP symbols remind students of the value of collaboration or persistence, skills they might have first encountered during a team-building exercise with their advisory group.

Still, raising Cristo Rey students' achievement takes more than introducing them to the mind-sets and skills that will help them figure out how to regulate their thoughts and emotions after years of damage to the prefrontal cortex. Duckworth breaks achievement down into motivation and volition. "What if students just aren't motivated to achieve the goals their teachers or parents want them to achieve?" Tough asks in his book. "Then, Duckworth acknowledges, all the self-control tricks in the world aren't going to help," he writes.[24] Students have to want to achieve.

FINDING THE DESIRE WITHIN

Something often clicks between sophomore and junior years of high school for Cristo Rey students. Christ the King junior Christopher Howard-Goodwin, for instance, went from failing two or three classes as a freshman to being on the honor roll. "He's somebody for whom it just came together, and he started working very hard and realized he can do it," says Pamela Rauscher, the dean of academics at the Newark school. Christopher is not the only success story. More than half of the students fail one class during freshman and sophomore years, says Rauscher, but only three juniors have failed a class in Christopher's year. Very few are required to go to Homework Center after school, and most of the class is now on the honor roll. Even the sophomores recognize the difference, hoping that they will be able to match their achievement in their junior year.

"The environment allows us to mature based on the work that they provide for us," Christopher says to explain the difference between sophomores and juniors. "We have to learn how to pick up those habits in order to succeed within the school. That's how life is."

The difference may come from two years of making mistakes and learning from them. Or it may come from the self-selection process that goes along with being a private school—Christopher's class is down to forty-three students from seventy-five by the end of the junior year. A big part, though, is that by junior year, the students have found their motivation. Life beyond high school is all of a sudden close.

Christopher's classmate Isabella Herrera also has struggled with academics throughout her time at Christ the King, Rauscher says. She has had to make up failed classes during summer school. As a freshman, she says, her attitude was, "I'll just do better next year." In the middle of junior year, students start a college guidance class that lasts through fall of their senior year. They learn the ins and outs of the college application process and work on their essays and applications. Isabella was nervous about starting the class. "I felt like, 'Wow, reality is hitting me,'" she says. "It was like a slap in the face: 'Wake up! You're growing up, and you have to learn how to figure your things out.' It was exciting, but it was more like a scary thrill."

Gone are the complaints about not being able to be yourself. All the rules and detentions that freshmen and sophomores hate have all of a sudden become relevant. "Now I see it as, if you don't want a detention, don't break the rules," Isabella says as her class-mates nod their heads in agreement. "Outside at work, they're not going to give you detentions; they're going to fire you."

Although Isabella, Christopher, and their classmates have come to understand both the goals and methodology of the Cristo Rey program in their third year at the school, the challenge for the schools is how to help students "get it" sooner. Sometimes Gebbia wishes he could have a fifth year with the students—they start to get it just as they are moving on from high school. Instead, though, the schools employ a variety of tactics to help keep goals such as college at the front of students' minds, even as they are starting high school.

Each Cristo Rey school is filled with physical reminders that students' goals should extend beyond high-school graduation. College pennants decorate the halls; schools post copies of every college acceptance letter that students receive. In Newark, a billboard announces how many scholarship dollars students have won. Teachers often bring college up in class. "As a college-ready student," a learning goal may begin. In the middle of a lesson on *The Great Gatsby,* an English teacher at Christ the King makes a point to emphasize that author F. Scott Fitzgerald went to Princeton—one of the best colleges in the country, she says.

Christ the King hosts a college fair at which schools set up information booths seeking to recruit students. The schools are primarily interested in talking to juniors and seniors, but underclassmen attend the college fair too. When they were young, the juniors say, they simply grabbed some brochures, confused by the variety of colleges. They did not understand that there were different types of colleges with different levels of selectivity and specializations. College was just the next step after high school, just as high school came after junior high. Grade point average and college application requirements were foreign ideas to them as well. Even if the school tried to teach them about college at that age, it did not sink in, Christopher says. As freshmen, they were still trying to adjust to a new high school, never mind thinking four years in advance.

The school has to help students find and name their aspirations, Gebbia says. Career awareness is an essential part of college readiness, according to David Conley's definition of "key transition knowledge and skills." High-school students must understand the various career paths they can take and the requirements for them as well as their own qualifications and interests. Gebbia and Rauscher believe strongly in taking students out of the classroom to help them find inspiration. "I wish I could have a $50,000 budget to go on little field trips, because it gives them a purpose for their learning," Gebbia says.

As at many Cristo Rey schools, many Christ the King students go to precollege immersion experiences—from Georgetown in Washington, DC, to Fairfield University in Connecticut. A benefactor sponsors twelve Christ the King students who have done well in biology to go to the Block Island Maritime Institute in Rhode Island. A number of female students from Christ the King go to the Girls' Career Institute at Douglass College on the campus of the University of Rutgers.

At the Girls' Career Institute, professional women talk about their careers and give college and career advice to students. Keisha Lane, a quiet African-American girl, was most interested in hearing a doctor talk about the college majors that are good for careers in medicine, the MCAT, and medical school. Keisha had long wanted to be a pediatric nurse, but she had never considered being a doctor. After doing some research, she elevated her goal to becoming a nurse practitioner, so that she could have more responsibilities, like having her own patients.

Keisha liked the career seminars, but she was more excited about having the chance to experience college life through the institute. She and the other girls lived in the dorms, staying up late and getting to know each other. "It was kind of weird because it was really my first time being away from my mom and my brothers," Keisha says. "I got used to it after the first two days."

Keisha hopes that college life is not all that different—the combination of fun activities and learning helpful information. She does not want to go too far away from home for college, but she does want to live on campus. "I want to get the full college experience. Living on campus, you get to meet new people and have different experiences," she says.

Even if students do not go off campus, the school can help them name their aspirations. Juniors start their school year with a Marking the Midpoint interview, an opportunity for students to reflect on where they have come from and where they still need to go. In the fifteen- to twenty-minute interviews, Gebbia and Rauscher help students formulate their personal, professional, and academic goals for after high school. The juniors also answer reflection questions prior to the interview. The prompts ask them about their motivations and dreams and encourage them to distinguish between unachievable fantasies and realistic dreams. The questions also ask what *ganas*—a Spanish term similar to "grit" used in many Cristo Rey schools—means to students, what qualities of the "Cristo Rey graduate at graduation" they have developed over the past two years, and what they still need to work on.

Keisha appreciated that Gebbia and Rauscher took a personal interest in who she is, how much she likes kids, and why she wants to become a nurse. "They really got to understand me," she says.

Isabella decided through the process that she wants to study journalism in college. It honored her that Rauscher, who worked as a broadcast journalist for seventeen years, took time out of her schedule to read some of her writing and provide feedback.

She and her classmates cannot say enough good things about Gebbia too. When students start as freshmen, they fear Gebbia. He jokes with them that the badges they wear around their necks every day contain chips that send him messages about where they are and what they are doing. Gebbia does not mind that they think he is omnipotent at first. Eventually, though, he wants them to understand that the school operates by the rule of law, not the rule of Father Greg. By the time they are juniors, the students have figured out that Gebbia is compassionate, sensitive, and funny. He takes time to interact with students on a personal level, playing games and cooking them dinner at SCAN. When Isabella's grandmother had a stroke, he and Sandoz visited her in the hospital. As priests, that pastoral care is a part of their daily lives, but it is special to the students.

"He looks strict, but if he sees you at a weak point, he comes to you personally and says, 'If you need me, my office is open to you whenever you need me.' He knows that if we're not good, we're not going to do good in class," Isabella says.

For some, the Marking the Midpoint process is about more than finding a long-term goal; it is also about finding that internal sense of self-worth—the man or woman of promise that drives them forward.

As a freshman and sophomore, Angela Duran earned a cumulative GPA of 1.668. For much of the first two years of high school, she admits that she dwelled on past mistakes and troubles instead of looking at her future possibilities. "I soon began to tell myself that there really was no point and that I wasn't as good as I thought I was," she wrote in her Marking the Midpoint essay.

During the summer before her junior year, she ran into one of her middle-school teachers, who asked her how she was doing. "I saw no reason to lie," she wrote. "After I told him how school was going, he simply told me, 'What are you doing?' and 'You are better than that.' Then I had to ask myself, 'What am I doing?' I knew I was better than this. I was smarter than the way I was acting, and I certainly wasn't a quitter. It was then that I felt some kind of enlightenment, I finally gained *ganas.* Without having the will or passion to be better, you feel you have no purpose, and with no purpose in life you have nothing to live for."

The first quarter of her junior year, Angela made second honors, which requires at least a 3.0 GPA.

The transformation from sophomore to junior year, though, does not mean the classes are any easier. Keisha struggled in honors math class much of her junior year. "I've cried, I've been stressed out. I have gone a week without eating because of math," she says. "I felt like, 'I don't care anymore. I just give up. I don't want to be here.'"

But when Keisha realized how many people were cheering for her to succeed, she knew she had to keep trying. "I had people around me, saying, 'You can't give up. That's not who you are,'" she says. It was more than just teachers, administrators, and friends; other classmates cheered her on too. There is a positive peer pressure that shapes the high-achieving culture of Cristo Rey schools, she and her classmates agree. On retreats, they get to know each other beyond high-school cliques and outward masks, and they want to see each other succeed.

The support encouraged Keisha to work harder in math, and she pulled her grade up from failing to a C in the last quarter. It was not enough to raise her cumulative grade; she ended up with a 70 percent—a D at Christ the King—for the year. After summer math enrichment, though, her math grade was at 80 percent for the first quarter of her senior year. "I'm at a school where they're not giving up on me, so why am I giving up on myself?" Keisha says.

An Ever-Widening Community

On a Friday in May, the multipurpose room at Verbum Dei is set up as a theater, with blue and yellow balloons tied to chairs and college pennants decorating the stage. The whole student body—except for students who are working—supporters, work sponsors, faculty, and staff are gathered for College Commitment Day. College signing day has never been an unusual event at Verbum Dei, which was a sports powerhouse known for producing NBA and NFL players before becoming a Cristo Rey school. But these days, College Commitment Day is not just for Verbum Dei athletes. All students celebrate their successful applications to college by making a public commitment to continue their education after high school.

Only a handful of family members are on hand. Lucia Rodriguez had to work extra hours on Thursday to get the time off to come to the ceremony. She sits with her dad, Emilio, a small frail man in a pinstripe suit, at the end of one row with a big bouquet of balloons for her son, Pablo Emilio Cabrera. Pablo's going to college is as important to her as his graduation from high school.

Principal Dan O'Connell gives a speech, reminding the seniors that, just as they have faced walls on their way to high-school graduation, there would be obstacles on their way to college graduation. They have the tools, though, to break through walls on their way to their goal, he says.

Then the boys rise one by one, walking up to the podium on the stage. They introduce themselves by name and work sponsor, announce where they plan to enroll in the fall, and sign their names and schools on a large yellow "Verbum Dei" sign behind them. Three announce together that they are going to Concordia University, holding up a T-shirt like a basketball jersey. Another student wears a St. John's sweatshirt to show off his choice of the Minnesota school. Another student unrolls a pennant. Many students announce community colleges. Everyone cheers hard when valedictorian Daniel Hall says he is going to Georgetown University. He remembers watching his role model announce Georgetown as his school a few years ago. Even then, Daniel could hardly wait for his moment onstage. College Commitment Day is as much an inspiration for underclassmen as it is a celebration for seniors.

When Pablo Cabrera climbs onstage to announce his college, he makes it to the podium, but does not say a word. Instead, he looks down and chokes up, putting his hand to his eyes. While the rest of the school looks on, first one, then five, and finally about ten seniors rush the stage and throw their arms around Pablo in a group hug, creating a ring of support around him. When they sit down again, Pablo announces with pride that he will be attending Cal State Dominguez Hills. Later he explains that he teared up onstage thinking of both the ups and the downs—the high points and the obstacles that O'Connell had talked about in his speech.

Pablo did not look the part of a Catholic school student when he started considering Verbum Dei. He had been growing his hair out since fourth grade, and going to a Catholic school would require him to cut it. By eighth grade Pablo also had given up on school. His grandmother had been sick throughout junior high, and when she passed away, it hit him hard. He was close to both his grandparents, despite the fact that his "dad," as he called his grandfather, had had a serious drinking problem. His grandfather is now sober and on dialysis. Pablo is proud to have his grandfather's name, Emilio, as his middle name.

Emilio has always wanted his children and grandchildren to be better off than he was, bringing them to the United States from Mexico to improve their lives. Pablo's mom, however, became a teen mom, ending her education after high school. For her kids, the first generation to be born in the United States, "There's no ifs, buts, or maybes" about college, Lucia Rodriguez says. "This is the way it's going to be. I need them to be able to support themselves."

Knowing his mom's desires for him, Pablo looked into Verbum Dei. He knew how hard she struggled having just a high-school degree and working multiple jobs to take care of him. And he appreciated the support and discipline that teachers provided at Verbum Dei. "They aren't as strict in public schools. They keep me on track here," he says.

Still, Pablo did not make friends with his classmates in his first few years at Verbum Dei. "I kept pushing everybody away from me," he says.

His home life also distracted him from school. He came home from work one day as a freshman to find out that his older cousin, a role model for Pablo and the only one in the family without legal status, was being held in a detention facility. A year later, he was deported, despite having been in the United States from age three. He had committed a crime in his teens, but had straightened out and become a father. While the cousin was in detention, another uncle passed away unexpectedly. Pablo was devastated, ready to give up on school again.

At the end of his sophomore year, though, he finally started making friends with some of his classmates. On his junior-year retreat, they all started talking about things nobody knew about each other, struggles they were going through and problems at home.

Senior year, Verbum Dei students go on a Kairos retreat—three days away from school, technology, and family. Pablo and his classmates expected that they'd just "chill" for three days, but the experience was more intense—from morning to late into the night they listened to each other's stories, reflected, and prayed. Pablo had never gotten along with one of his classmates, but when he heard the other boy's story of personal struggles at Kairos, Pablo found that they had a lot in common. He got up and publicly apologized for misjudging his classmate. "The Kairos retreat was basically the biggest life-changing thing for me," Pablo says. "The retreat brought out this religious part of me that I had no idea was in me."

The reflective nature of Catholic education—and school retreats specifically—give students the opportunity to reflect on big questions about God, relationships, and the meaning of one's life. Even students who are not Catholic or religious appreciate the time and space to be reflective. But retreats are not only time for individual reflection; they also bring together classmates in a community to serve others.

The Cristo Rey spirituality centers on Jesus. By developing a relationship with Jesus, students come to understand God's love for them, which in turn drives them to love each other. On their first day at the all-boys school, O'Connell tells the freshmen that they are brothers, but it takes some time for that to sink in. With each year of retreats, students become closer, and it hurts if one of the brothers leaves the school, Verbum Dei campus minister Karen Chambers says. They support each other. Pablo, for instance, found a friend who helps him keep his faith during hard times. "Do you see how you always end up getting back to religion when you need help?" his friend would ask him. "He helped me realize the person who I really came to be," Pablo says.

And that person is the type who tries to donate a kidney to his grandfather, so he would not need dialysis anymore (his grandfather was too frail to undergo the surgery). Having gone through counseling, Pablo wants to become a psychiatrist. He simply wants to help people, Pablo says, before going off to volunteer with elementary-school students who come to Verbum Dei's campus for tutoring and after-school activities.

The love that students feel is directed into service opportunities. Students are called to give back as a way of coming to know God better, an idea rooted in the Bible. In feeding the hungry, clothing the naked, and caring for the ill, Jesus's followers feed, clothe, and care for him. "Amen, I say to you, whatever you did for one of these least brothers and sisters of mine, you did for me," Jesus says (Matt. 25:40).

Verbum Dei has a service requirement, with after-school and Saturday service opportunities, but other unique events also inspire students to give back. As his freshman year at Verbum Dei comes to a close, Miguel Rios counts Homelessness Awareness Week as one of the highlights of his year. He and his classmates slept under the stars at Verbum Dei to find out what it might be like to have to sleep outside, and they listened to a speaker talk about how she slept in her car while putting herself through college. Miguel also was impressed to hear a presentation from students who went to a Navajo reservation to work with people with mental disabilities over spring break. In addition to the spring break trip, Verbum Dei takes students to the Ignatian Family Teach-In, a national gathering of Jesuit high-school and university groups with social justice workshops. Some Cristo Rey schools take their students on international service trips to Africa or Central America as well.

Whether or not students recognize their family's own economic status, serving others offers a valuable lesson. "Nobody is helpless," Chambers says. "No matter where you are, no matter whether you have high income, low income, middle income, no matter your age even, everybody can make a difference. Everybody can stand in solidarity with others, work to bring about more justice, and do some service."

Coming Full Circle

Andy Laureano, associate director of college initiatives at the Cristo Rey Network, can relate to the ups and downs that Pablo experienced in high school. Laureano grew up on a street between two gang territories not far from the original Cristo Rey school in Chicago. He did not feel safe at his elementary school, which was overcrowded and frequently went on lockdown. "It looked like an ant farm at 3:30—hundreds of students spilling out of one building," Laureano says. Neighbors asked him to join their gang in junior high. After school one day, his house was shot at in a drive-by. He wanted his mom to be around that night, but she had to leave for work before his dad came home from work. Laureano still remembers his dad cooking him Cup O' Noodles soup for dinner that night. Life went on as if such an occurrence was normal. Laureano believed that he would be in a gang or dead by his mid-twenties.

As an eighth grader, Laureano showed up to his Cristo Rey interview in jeans and work boots, but the high school gave him a chance to change his path. Thanks to the school, Laureano has not only survived; he has thrived. Before his ten-year high-school reunion, Laureano found a job he loves and married his college girlfriend. He and his wife, Martha, bought a dog and a nicely re-habbed bungalow, complete with granite countertops, in a suburb just west of Chicago.

Even in his twenties, Laureano clearly remembers his graduation from Cristo Rey Jesuit in Chicago. Father James Gartland, SJ, who had conducted the feasibility study for the original school back in 1993, was president of the school when Laureano graduated in 2006. "He said, 'Don't forget about the community. Come back to us. You're graduating from your home,'" Laureano recalls. "For me, that resonates a lot even to this day. How can I push myself to do better for my community?"

Though he has moved out of his neighborhood, Laureano remains committed to serving his community. He works on the weekends with a nonprofit that helps high-school students work toward college. He is also on the board of a domestic violence nonprofit serving his old neighborhood. His job at the Cristo Rey Network required him to take a pay cut from his previous position. His parents could not understand why he would take it, but for him the Cristo Rey position was a calling and a way to give back.

His job at the Cristo Rey Network includes reaching out to fellow alumni to find out how the Network can serve them best and help them find success in college. Often, alumni come back and ask how they can help their schools and current students.

At the Network's University Partners, Cristo Rey alumni are finding ways to serve each other and others, just as they did in high school. Loyola University Chicago set up a Cristo Rey Scholars program, giving full-ride scholarships to a handful of Cristo Rey graduates each year. Loyola has fifty-four Cristo Rey graduates studying at the school. The Cristo Rey scholars have shaped their own program, asking for grade requirements and mandated study sessions for underclassmen. They set up a mentoring program for new Cristo Rey graduates who come to Loyola and coordinate activities for the group. Cristo Rey students might go kayaking together or visit Chicago landmarks, but just as often they are looking for service opportunities at their new school.

Melissa Foy, executive director of the Georgetown Scholarship Program, has seen the same phenomenon at Georgetown, where fifty-seven Cristo Rey graduates attend. Her scholarship program covers students coming from all types of high schools, but the Cristo Rey students are the most involved. Instead of coming to her for services, Cristo Rey alumni come to her to ask how they can help. When it is new-student week, they will help pick up students at the airport and get them settled into their dorms, knowing how difficult it is to show up on campus without family. They start coat drives for the homeless in the middle of the winter— and Foy has to make sure they do not give away their own winter coats. "They give back ten times what they get," Foy says. "I think a lot of it is, 'I want to bring my high school up, my community up, my family up. This isn't just an education for me; I want to serve as a positive role model.'"

With the desire to serve, a college degree, and professional skills, Cristo Rey alumni will have plenty of opportunities to give back to the wider community. Cristo Rey Boston board member Hugh McLaughlin is confident about that. He sees his own family's story in the students the school serves. "Whether you're coming from the coasts of Ireland or Italy or Haiti or Somalia, you're first generation," McLaughlin says.

His grandfather, Hughie, came to the United States as a sixteen-year-old orphan with nothing. Today, his family construction company, Sullivan & McLaughlin, employs more than five hundred people and is a corporate work-study sponsor for Cristo Rey Boston. The immigrant students he met on his first trip to the school convinced him that he needed to be involved. Still, McLaughlin had no idea how big of an impact his first work-study student, Jose Luis Vargas, would have on him.

Jose and his mother emigrated from the Dominican Republic, and when he turns eighteen after high school, Jose could bring his father to Boston as well. Jose shakes your hand and makes good eye contact; he is open and honest, engaged, optimistic, and mature beyond his years, McLaughlin says. The development chair of the Cristo Rey Boston board, McLaughlin hosted a breakfast fund-raiser with about seventy-five of the "who's who of Boston" when Jose was a sophomore. "We threw Jose at the podium, totally unprepared, off the cuff, and he crushed it— absolutely phenomenal job," McLaughlin says. Jose, he brags, is graduating fifth in his class and earned a four-year scholarship to Northeastern University.

McLaughlin and Jose first started getting close while talking over lunch. McLaughlin started taking him along on work-site visits, and he would ask Jose about classes, tests, and basketball games. During his junior year, McLaughlin had him bring five out-of-state colleges that he had researched into work with him every week. "All of a sudden you get bought into what he's doing, like your own kid," McLaughlin says.

On one work-site visit, McLaughlin surprised Jose by asking him to drive. He had just gotten his learner's permit, having missed a driver's education class at school due to basketball season.

"I learned how to drive the old-fashioned way," Jose jokes, "your parents—or your boss. This man is like a father figure to me," he says seriously.

When Jose first said this to him, "it kind of blew me away," McLaughlin says. "It's pretty cool for that to happen. It doesn't take much. For a kid who doesn't have it, even a little bit means a lot."

McLaughlin's Ford F-150 fits a construction company executive, but Jose, a lanky teenager, almost looks comical climbing into its high cab. He grips the steering wheel as he slowly rolls down a quiet road, trying to make casual conversation with McLaughlin along the way.

"Did you ever work in the field?" Jose asks, when McLaughlin points out a solar site the company has worked on.

"I still have my work belt. My skills are more in talking and sales than mechanics," McLaughlin replies between instructions about how to merge onto a busier street. Jose waits until the road is completely clear before proceeding.

McLaughlin points to a yellow building that houses a muffler shop. That is where his father started Sullivan & McLaughlin, he says. He flashes back to his own teen years, driving down the same streets with his grandfather. His grandfather, Hughie, essentially raised him and was his best friend growing up. He would have wanted his grandson to be involved with an organization like Cristo Rey, two generations later, McLaughlin says.

There is "a little bit of the American story to it," McLaughlin explains. Cristo Rey gives students like Jose the opportunity to earn a living, have a house, and drive a car. "All the little basic things that we all should have in this country, he'll be able to do now."

But there is more to McLaughlin's American Dream than taking care of yourself. He is already recruiting Jose for when he graduates from Northeastern University—not necessarily to work in the construction industry, but for Cristo Rey Boston. "He'll be sitting on the board with me someday," McLaughlin smiles.

Acknowledgments

When I asked people at the annual Cristo Rey Network meeting how they ended up working with Cristo Rey, many said that their stories were providential. My story is as well. As a high-school student, I volunteered in Chicago's Pilsen neighborhood, just blocks away from the young original Cristo Rey school. Not all students, I found, have access to excellent public schools, as I did in the suburbs.

After college, I volunteered at a charter school just three miles from Cristo Rey Jesuit High School in Pilsen through Amate House, a full-time Catholic volunteer program. I watched the charter school's basketball team handily beat Cristo Rey's team in their brand-new gym. I also played basketball with Cristo Rey's full-time volunteers in that gym. A few years later, I returned to the gym again, this time as an editor at *U.S. Catholic* magazine celebrating the graduation of our excellent student worker.

I would be remiss to not thank all of those who helped expose me to urban education and shape my career: my fellow Amate House volunteers, Jeff McCarter of Free Spirit Media, John Horan of North Lawndale College Preparatory Charter High School, the students with whom I worked, and my fellow editors at *U.S. Catholic*.

David Gibson, a journalist for whom I have the utmost respect, was not aware of my connections to Cristo Rey when he gave my name to his editor, Roger Freet of HarperOne, as a potential writer for this book. I cannot thank David enough for thinking of me, and Roger and Father Robert Sandoz for giving me the opportunity to write about an organization that I have followed since high school. Thank you to both Roger and editorial assistant Hilary Lawson for their edits and guidance while writing the book. And thanks to attorney John Munro of Vedder Price for help with the contract, and Milton Wood and Jack Obiala for connecting me to John.

As president of Christ the King Preparatory School in Newark, New Jersey, Father Sandoz not only helped initiate this book project; he also opened his school to me. I am grateful to all the other schools that did so as well. Father William Muller, SJ, and his team allowed me to spend a significant amount of time at Verbum Dei High School in Los Angeles. From visits with future students to a board meeting, Jeff Thielman and the Cristo Rey Boston High School team gave me full access to their school. AmeriCorps volunteers Doug McNicol, Laura Capasso, Rosie Miola, and William Brown were gracious hosts in Boston. Father T. J. Martinez, SJ, and everyone involved with Cristo Rey Jesuit

College Preparatory School in Houston made time for me in the midst of a hectic graduation week. I also toured Cristo Rey Jesuit High School–Twin Cities and the original Cristo Rey Jesuit in Chicago. At Cristo Rey St. Martin College Prep in Waukegan, Illinois, Preston Kendall shared insights about both the school and the Network.

I am especially appreciative of all teachers, administrators, board members, donors, students, alumni, and their families who let me into their lives and helped bring life to the book. I collected many more stories than can be told in these pages, but all helped shape the writing of this book.

Thanks also to the education experts who helped me understand the larger context of the Cristo Rey Network's work and to Cristo Rey Network personnel who patiently helped me understand the ins and outs of curriculum design and the corporate work-study program. Thanks especially to Jack Crowe, Brenda Schulze, Randy Kurtz, former CEO Rob Birdsell, Father John Foley, SJ, Elizabeth Goettl, Chris Broughton, Ken Malik, and Andy and Martha Laureano.

Spending time in high schools makes you reflect on your own high-school experience. I have come to realize that my teachers were the creative and thoughtful educators every child deserves. My thanks go to all of the educators who have helped me get where I am, especially my journalism professors at Northwestern University and University of Southern California. I remember learning at Medill that journalism is the career for lifelong learners, and I knew I had found my calling. Thank you to the professors and mentors who have supported me in my career.

In writing this book, I also learned how important family is to life outcomes. I have to thank my parents, Shar Barron and Jerry Sweas, for instilling in me the curiosity and drive—the grit, in other words—needed to write a book. Thank you to all of my family and friends for their support and encouragement, especially Jason and Kate Sweas and Brad Weyers. Thanks to Abby Wolbe for hosting me in the midst of a reporting trip and to my many teacher friends for sharing their thoughts on education with me. Finally, thank you to my nephews, Jack and Sam, for providing me with happy distractions from my work.

Appendix A:
Mission Effectiveness Standards

As a member of the Cristo Rey Network, a school:

1. Is explicitly Catholic in mission and enjoys Church approval.
2. Serves only economically disadvantaged students. The school is open to students of various faiths and cultures.
3. Is family centered and plays an active role in the local community.
4. Shall prepare all of its students to enter and graduate from college.
5. Requires participation by all students in the work-study program. All students must be fourteen years old by September 1.
6. Integrates the learning present in its work program, classroom, and extracurricular experiences for the fullest benefit of its student workers.

7. Has an effective administrative and board structure as well as complies with all applicable state and federal laws.

8. Is financially sound and at full enrollment is primarily dependent on revenue from the work-study program to meet operating expenses. In addition, the school maintains a comprehensive advancement program to ensure financial stability.

9. Supports its graduates' efforts to obtain a college degree.

10. Is an active participant in the collaboration, support, and development of the Cristo Rey Network.

Appendix B:
Techniques and Resources

As Elizabeth Goettl explains, the methods that Cristo Rey teachers use in the classroom are not unusual, but represent best practices. Below are some of the defining characteristics of the Network's Teach-Learn-Lead program:

Teach

Professional Development: The Network's summer professional development for teachers trains them in the Network curriculum, lesson planning, instructional shifts, and high-impact instructional strategies.

Schools also continue professional development throughout the year, often led by principals, deans of instruction and/or academics, and master teachers. Many organize teachers into small learning communities. Numerous schools put in place a rounds-like system allowing teachers to observe and learn from each other without administration or an evaluative component.

Instructional Shifts: In order to promote literacy, all teachers are expected to work with students on reading and communicating within various domains. Network professional development helps science, math, social studies, and religious studies teachers work on the following six instructional shifts:

1. A balance of literary and informational texts
2. Literacy across all content areas
3. Increasing complexity of texts
4. Text-based questions and answers
5. Writing using evidence
6. Academic vocabulary

High-Impact Instructional Strategies: These teaching strategies are used to engage all students in a classroom, and because all teachers are trained in them, there is consistency across classrooms in a school and across the Network.

Resources: Robert Marzano (http://www.marzanoresearch.com/) has provided professional development to teachers. Teachers also use Doug Lemov's *Teach Like a Champion: 49 Techniques That*

Put Students on the Path to College (San Francisco: Jossey-Bass, 2010); see also http://teachlikeachampion.com.

Learn

The Cristo Rey Network curriculum is based on research on what a student needs to know and be able to do to succeed in college. The following resources are essential to the curriculum development:

Common Core State Standards: The Cristo Rey Network Curriculum is aligned with the Common Core. Learn more at http://www.corestandards.org/.

ACT College and Career Readiness Standards: The Cristo Rey Network Curriculum is also aligned with the ACT standards. Learn more at https://www.act.org/standard/.

For David Conley's model of College and Career Readiness, see http://www.epiconline.org/Issues/college-career-readiness/the-solution/.

For Partnership for 21st Century Skills' Framework for 21st Century Learning, see http://www.p21.org/our-work/p21-framework.

Lead

Principals are given professional development assistance to become academic leaders rather than school managers. The Network encourages principals to visit each teacher's classroom once a week, basing evaluations on short, frequent visits rather than one full class period of observation. The Network has trained principals in Charlotte Danielson's framework for effective teaching, which divides a teacher's work into four domains:

1. Planning and Preparation
2. Classroom Environment
3. Instruction
4. Professional Responsibilities

For more information on the framework, visit http://www.danielsongroup.org.

Character Development

Cristo Rey Network's character development program is rooted in the Catholic faith and the tradition of *cura personalis,* or care for the entire person. Religious offerings include daily prayer, school Masses, retreats, campus ministry, after-school volunteer programs, and service trips.

Character formation, however, need not be limited to Catholic education, and there are many lessons that nonreligious educators can take from Cristo Rey schools. All schools can create a community around a shared vision—which starts with the adults—and help students realize their true identity and worth. Here are some of the resources and tools that Cristo Rey schools use:

Grit: University of Pennsylvania researcher Angela Lee Duckworth's website provides articles about how grit and self-control help achievement and about opportunities for educators to get involved in her project; see https://sites.sas.upenn.edu/duckworth/pages/educators.

Growth Mind-Set: Cristo Rey schools also teach their students to have a growth mind-set—the belief that intelligence is malleable. Stanford University professor Carol Dweck's book *Mindset: The New Psychology of Success* (New York: Ballantine, 2006) shares how mind-set affects achievement; see also http://mind-setonline.com.

APPs: Developed by Cristo Rey Jesuit Preparatory School in Houston, the APPs provide students with visual reminders of cognitive skills that they can work on in class or at work:

Teamwork and Collaboration: *image of hands linked*

Precision and Accuracy: *image of an arrow and target*

Persistence: *image of a small figure pushing a large sphere*

Complex Reasoning Strategies: *image of a head with an active, colorful brain*

Initiative and Self-Direction: *image of a curvy road and compass*

Productivity and Accountability: *image of an upward-trending graph*

For a summary of the research on character skills, read Paul Tough's *How Children Succeed: Grit, Curiosity, and the Hidden Power of Character* (Boston: Houghton Mifflin Harcourt, 2012); see also http://www.paultough.com/the-books/how-children-succeed/.

Notes

INTRODUCTION: BREAKTHROUGHS IN A BROKEN SYSTEM

1. "Jones High School," *Public School Explorer,* accessed March 9, 2014, http://www.texastribune.org/public-ed/explore/houston-isd/jones -high-school/#college-readiness.
2. G. R. Kearney, *More Than a Dream: The Cristo Rey Story: How One School's Vision Is Changing the World* (Chicago: Loyola, 2008), Kindle edition, location 168–88.
3. Kearney, *More Than a Dream,* location 876–83.
4. Kearney, *More Than a Dream,* location 1230.
5. Lawrence W. Lezotte, "Revolutionary and Evolutionary: The Effective School Movement," accessed March 5, 2014, http://www .edutopia.org/pdfs/cdutopia.org-closing achievement-gap-lezotte -article.pdf.

CHAPTER ONE: THE CHALLENGE OF INNER-CITY EDUCATION

1. "School History," Cristo Rey Boston High School, accessed March 5, 2014, http://www.cristoreyboston.org/school-history.
2. "2013 Snapshot Report: Student Profile," Cristo Rey Network Annual Data Report 2013, 5.

3. "2013 Snapshot Report: Student Profile," Cristo Rey Network Annual Data Report 2013, 5.

4. "U.S. Catholics: Key Data from Pew Research," Pew Research Center, February 25, 2013, http://www.pewresearch.org/key-data -points/u-s-catholics-key-data-from-pew-research/#popsize; "United States Catholic Elementary and Secondary Schools 2013–2014: The Annual Statistical Report on Schools, Enrollment, and Staffing," National Catholic Education Association, accessed March 5, 2014, http:// www.ncea.org/data-information/catholic-school-data.

5. Richard Fry and Kim Parker, "Record Shares of Young Adults Have Finished Both High School and College," Pew Research Social & Demographic Trends, November 5, 2012, http://www.pewsocialtrends .org/2012/11/05/record-shares-of-young-adults-have-finished-both -high-school-and-college/.

6. Fry and Parker, "Record Shares."

7. John H. Tyler and Magnus Lofstrom, "Finishing High School: Alternative Pathways and Dropout Recovery," *The Future of Children* 19, no. 1 (Spring 2009): 82.

8. Sean F. Reardon, "No Rich Child Left Behind," *New York Times,* April 27, 2013, http://opinionator.blogs.nytimes.com/2013/04/27/no -rich-child-left-behind/.

9. Robert Balfanz, "Can the American High School Become an Avenue of Advancement for All?" *The Future of Children* 19, no. 1 (Spring 2009): 22.

10. Balfanz, "Can the American High School Become an Avenue of Advancement for All?": 22.

11. "Earnings and Unemployment Rates by Educational Attainment," Bureau of Labor Statistics, accessed April 7, 2014, http://bls.gov/emp /ep_chart_001.htm.

12. "Earnings and Unemployment Rates by Educational Attainment."

13. David T. Conley, *Getting Ready for College, Careers, and the Common Core: What Every Educator Needs to Know* (San Francisco: Jossey-Bass, 2014), 25.

14. Peter R. Orszag, "The Diploma Gap Between Rich and Poor,"

Bloomberg View, March 5, 2013, http://www.bloomberg.com/news/2013-03-05/the-diploma-gap-between-rich-and-poor.html.

15. "Remedial Education: Federal Education Policy," Council on Foreign Relations, June 2013, http://www.cfr.org/united-states/remedial-education-federal-education-policy/p30141.

16. "U.S. Education Reform and National Security," Council on Foreign Relations, March 2012, http://www.cfr.org/united-states/us-education-reform-national-security/p27618.

17. Balfanz, "Can the American High School Become an Avenue of Advancement for All?": 27.

18. "North Cambridge Catholic High School to Move to Dorchester," Archdiocese of Boston, accessed March 5, 2014, http://www.bostoncatholic.org/Utility/News-And-Press/Content.aspx?id=16720.

19. Interview with Thomas Hunt, March 18, 2013.

20. Anthony S. Bryk, Valerie E. Lee, and Peter B. Holland, *Catholic Schools and the Common Good* (Cambridge, MA: Harvard Univ. Press, 1993), 101–2.

21. Bryk, Lee, and Holland, *Catholic Schools and the Common Good,* 101.

22. Bryk, Lee, and Holland, *Catholic Schools and the Common Good,* 31.

23. Bryk, Lee, and Holland, *Catholic Schools and the Common Good,* 31.

24. "O'Neill, Thomas Philip, Jr. (Tip), (1912–1994)," Biographical Directory of the United States Congress, accessed March 5, 2014 http://bioguide.congress.gov/scripts/biodisplay.pl?index=o000098.

25. "North Cambridge Catholic High School to Move to Dorchester."

26. Reardon, "No Rich Child Left Behind."

27. Bryk, Lee, and Holland, *Catholic Schools and the Common Good,* 58.

28. Bryk, Lee, and Holland, *Catholic Schools and the Common Good,* 75–76.

29. Bryk, Lee, and Holland, *Catholic Schools and the Common Good,* 116.

30. Bryk, Lee, and Holland, *Catholic Schools and the Common Good,* 104.

31. Bryk, Lee, and Holland, *Catholic Schools and the Common Good,* 75–76.

32. Bryk, Lee, and Holland, *Catholic Schools and the Common Good,* 34.

33. "United States Catholic Elementary and Secondary Schools 2013–2014: The Annual Statistical Report on Schools, Enrollment, and Staffing," National Catholic Education Association.

34. Bryk, Lee, and Holland, *Catholic Schools and the Common Good,* 34.

35. E-mail from Matt Russell, Executive Director for Secondary Schools, National Catholic Education Association, December 9, 2013.

36. Numbers include both primary and secondary schools. In the 2013–14 school year, secondary schools enrolled 582,785 ("United States Catholic Elementary and Secondary Schools 2013–2014").

37. Jeff Thielman, "School Turnaround: Cristo Rey Boston High School Case Study," *Catholic Education: A Journal of Inquiry and Practice* 16, no. 1 (September 2012): 124.

38. Thielman, "School Turnaround," 126.

39. Thielman, "School Turnaround," 126.

40. Thielman, "School Turnaround," 127.

41. Thielman, "School Turnaround," 128–29.

42. Thielman, "School Turnaround," 127, 130.

43. Thielman, "School Turnaround," 130–31.

44. Thielman, "School Turnaround," 134.

45. Thielman, "School Turnaround," 135.

46. "Academic Success: Key Performance Indicator #1: ACT Gains" and "Academic Success: Key Performance Indicator #3: College Enrollment," Cristo Rey Network Annual Data Report 2013, 39, 41.

47. Thielman, "School Turnaround," 137; "Table 5: Admissions Analysis: Class of 2017 Family Income 2013–2014," Cristo Rey Annual Data Report 2013: 63.

CHAPTER TWO: A NEW VISION OF ADMINISTRATION

1. G. R. Kearney, *More Than a Dream: The Cristo Rey Story: How One School's Vision Is Changing the World* (Chicago: Loyola, 2008), Kindle edition, location 1203.

2. Kearney, *More Than a Dream,* location 689.

3. John T. James, "A Research-Based Approach to the President-Principal Model: Problems, Dynamics, and High Performance Through Administrative Alignment," *Catholic Education: A Journal of Inquiry and Practice* 12, no. 3 (March 2009): 400.

4. Anthony S. Bryk, Valerie E. Lee, and Peter B. Holland, *Catholic Schools and the Common Good* (Cambridge, MA: Harvard Univ. Press, 1993), 150–51.
5. Bryk, Lee, and Holland, *Catholic Schools and the Common Good,* 164, 336.
6. James, "A Research-Based Approach," 400.
7. James, "A Research-Based Approach," 399–400.
8. William Dygert, C.S.C., "The President/Principal Model in Catholic Secondary Schools," *Catholic Education: A Journal of Inquiry and Practice* 4, no. 1 (September 2000): 33.
9. "Lessons Learned from the First Decade," Cristo Rey Network, 2012.
10. Dygert, "The President/Principal Model," 18.
11. "Table 13: Composition of All Faculty & Staff 2012–2013," Cristo Rey Annual Data Report 2012, 42.
12. Antonio Ortiz is president, Patricia Garrity is the principal, and Jose Rodriguez is the corporate work-study director.
13. "Lessons Learned from the First Decade," Cristo Rey Network.
14. Kearney, *More Than a Dream,* location 1471.
15. Kearney, *More Than a Dream,* location 2390.
16. Kearney, *More Than a Dream,* location 1959.
17. "Mapping L.A.: Watts," *Los Angeles Times,* accessed March 5, 2014, http://maps.latimes.com/neighborhoods/neighborhood/watts/.
18. Bryk, Lee, and Holland, *Catholic Schools and the Common Good,* 223.
19. "Table 18: Faculty Salary Information 2012–2013," Cristo Rey Network Annual Data Report, Fall 2012: 49.
20. "Voucher Payment Standards," Housing Authority of the City of Los Angeles, updated March 1, 2014, http://www.hacla.org/vchr/.
21. Sid Garcia, "Occupancy, Rent on the Rise in Southland," ABC 7 News, January 23, 2013, http://abclocal.go.com/kabc/story?section=news/state&id=8966016.
22. "Table 17: Faculty Salary Information 2013–2014," Cristo Rey Network Annual Data Report, Fall 2013, 78.
23. "Table 18: Faculty Salary Information 2012–2013," Cristo Rey Network Annual Data Report Fall, 2012, 49.

24. "Table 16: Faculty Experience and Background 2013–2014," Cristo Rey Network Annual Data Report, Fall 2013, 77.

25. Kearney, *More Than a Dream,* location 1164.

26. Kearney, *More Than a Dream,* location 1157.

27. Kearney, *More Than a Dream,* location 1684–1705.

28. "Table 11: HR Analysis: Full-Time Equivalent (FTE) Faculty/Staff and Student Ratios 2013–2014," Cristo Rey Network Annual Data Report 2013, 70.

CHAPTER THREE: FROM ONE SCHOOL TO MANY:
BUILDING A NETWORK OF SUPPORT

1. G. R. Kearney, *More Than a Dream: The Cristo Rey Story: How One School's Vision Is Changing the World* (Chicago: Loyola, 2008), Kindle edition, location 2594.

2. Kearney, *More Than a Dream,* location 2634.

3. Kearney, *More Than a Dream,* location 2756.

4. Kearney, *More Than a Dream,* location 3343.

5. Kearney, *More Than a Dream,* location 3331.

6. Kearney, *More Than a Dream,* location 3357.

7. Kearney, *More Than a Dream,* location 3376.

8. Kearney, *More Than a Dream,* location 2949.

9. "The Cristo Rey Network: An Historical Profile," Cristo Rey Network, August 2011, 30.

10. "The Cristo Rey Network: An Historical Profile," 29.

11. Lisa Maxson, "Beginning at the End," *Catholic Voice,* May 18, 2007, http://catholicvoiceomaha.com/beginning-end-0.

12. Christopher Burbach, "School's Closing Stuns Students," *Omaha World-Herald,* February 12, 2011, http://www.omaha.com/article/20110212/NEWS01/702129875.

13. "Replication Process," Cristo Rey Network, November 2012.

14. "ACT College Readiness Benchmarks," ACT, accessed March 5, 2014, http://www.act.org/solutions/college-career-readiness/college-readiness-benchmarks/.

CHAPTER FOUR: LIFELONG LEARNERS

1. G. R. Kearney, *More Than a Dream: The Cristo Rey Story: How One School's Vision Is Changing the World* (Chicago: Loyola, 2008), Kindle edition, location 2834.

2. Kearney, *More Than a Dream,* location 2841.

3. David T. Conley, *Getting Ready for College, Careers, and the Common Core: What Every Educator Needs to Know* (San Francisco: Jossey-Bass, 2014), 33.

4. Valerie E. Lee and Douglas D. Ready, "U.S. High School Curriculum: Three Phases of Contemporary Research and Reform," *The Future of Children* 19, no. 1 (Spring 2009): 143.

5. Lee and Ready, "U.S. High School Curriculum," 139.

6. Conley, *Getting Ready for College,* 30.

7. Conley, *Getting Ready for College,* 143.

8. National Governors Association Center for Best Practices and Council of Chief State School Officers, *Common Core State Standards,* CCSS.ELA Literacy.W.K.2, CCSS.ELA Literacy.W.3.2, & CCSS .ELA-Literacy.W.11–12.2 (Washington, DC: 2010).

9. David Conley, interview with the author, July 7, 2013.

10. Al Baker, "Common Core Curriculum Now Has Critics on the Left," *New York Times,* February 16, 2014, accessed February 25, 2014, http://www.nytimes.com/2014/02/17/nyregion/new -york-early-champion-of-common-core-standards-joins-critics .html?emc=eta1.

11. Neal McCluskey, "You Aren't a Total Kook if You Oppose Common Core," *Cato Institute,* accessed March 5, 2014, http://www.cato .org/publications/commentary/you-arent-total-kook-you-oppose -common-core.

12. Lee and Ready, "U.S. High School Curriculum," 145–47.

13. Lee and Ready, "U.S. High School Curriculum," 150.

14. Conley, interview with the author, July 7, 2013.

15. Conley, *Getting Ready for College,* 19–20.

16. Conley, *Getting Ready for College,* 116.

17. Paul Tough, *How Children Succeed: Grit, Curiosity, and the Hidden Power of Character* (Boston: Houghton Mifflin Harcourt, 2012), 97.

18. National Governors Association Center for Best Practices and Council of Chief State School Officers, *Common Core State Standards,* CCSS.MATH.PRACTICE.MP1.

19. Tom Corcoran and Megan Silander, "Instruction in High Schools: The Evidence and the Challenge," *The Future of Children* 19, no. 1 (Spring 2009): 173–74.

20. Corcoran and Silander, "Instruction in High Schools," 174.

21. Corcoran and Silander, "Instruction in High Schools," 174.

22. "College Readiness Benchmark Attainment by State," 2013 ACT National and State Scores, accessed March 5, 2014, https://www.act .org/newsroom/data/2013/benchmarks.html.

23. National Governors Association Center for Best Practices, *Common Core State Standards,* English Language Arts, Appendix A, 3.

24. Corcoran and Silander, "Instruction in High Schools," 172.

25. National Governors Association Center for Best Practices, *Common Core State Standards,* "English Language Arts Standards Introduction, Key Design Considerations."

26. Susan Ryan, "Balancing the Common Core: The Truth About Informational Text," McREL Blog, August 13, 2013, http://blog .mcrel.org/2013/08/balancing-the-common-core-the-truth-about -informational-text.html.

27. Jeff Thielman, "School Turnaround: Cristo Rey Boston High School Case Study," *Catholic Education: A Journal of Inquiry and Practice* 16, no. 1 (September 2012): 128.

28. Note: For the Spanish Language and Spanish Literature AP tests, 88 and 80 percent of students, respectively, scored 3 or better. Other tests range from 0 percent earning a 3 or higher, to 56 percent of a nine-person AP World History class in Baltimore. "Table 22: AP Course Offerings and Test Participation 2012–2013," Cristo Rey Network Annual Data Report 2013, 82.

29. Conley, interview with the author, July 7, 2013.

30. "California State University–Dominguez Hills," College Results Online, accessed March 12, 2014, http://collegeresults.org/college profile.aspx?institutionid=110547.

CHAPTER FIVE: A WORK-PROGRAM REVOLUTION

1. "Table 45: Corporate Work Study: Current Year 2013–2014," Cristo Rey Network Annual Data Report 2013, 116.
2. "Research Brief: Dynamics of How Work-Based Learning Influences Youth Who Are at Higher Risk of Underachievement," Search Institute, June 2011, 2–4.
3. "School History," Cristo Rey Boston High School.
4. "Research Brief: Dynamics of How Work-Based Learning Influences Youth," 5.
5. "Table 9: 9th Grade Transfers, Withdrawals & Dismissals: Why Students Left and Where They Went Between October 1, 2012, and September 30, 2013" and "Table 10: 10th–12th Grade Transfers, Withdrawals & Dismissals: Why Students Left and Where They Went Between October 1, 2012, and September 30, 2013," Cristo Rey Network Annual Data Report 2013, 67–68.
6. G. R. Kearney, *More Than a Dream: The Cristo Rey Story: How One School's Vision Is Changing the World* (Chicago: Loyola, 2008), Kindle edition, location 1598.
7. "Table 44: Corporate Work Study: Prior Year 2011–2012," Cristo Rey Network Annual Data Report 2012, 84.
8. "Table 44: Corporate Work Study: Prior Year 2011–2012."

CHAPTER SIX: FAITH AND GRIT

1. Anthony S. Bryk, Valerie E. Lee, and Peter B. Holland, *Catholic Schools and the Common Good* (Cambridge, MA: Harvard Univ. Press, 1993), 317.
2. Bryk, Lee, and Holland, *Catholic Schools and the Common Good,* 144.
3. "Our Work," Duckworth Lab, University of Pennsylvania, accessed March 5, 2014, https://sites.sas.upenn.edu/duckworth.
4. Angela Lee Duckworth, "True Grit: Can Perseverance Be Taught?" *TEDx Talks,* uploaded on November 12, 2009, http://www.youtube.com/watch?v=qaeFnxSfSC4.
5. Angela Lee Duckworth, "The Key to Success? Grit," *TED Talks Education,* filmed April 2013, http://www.ted.com/talks/angela_lee_duckworth_the_key_to_success_grit.html.

6. Paul Tough, *How Children Succeed: Grit, Curiosity, and the Hidden Power of Character* (Boston: Houghton Mifflin Harcourt, 2012), 59.

7. Tables 9 and 10, Cristo Rey Network Annual Data Report 2013, 67–68. Note: The numbers do not add to 100 because schools do not know why some students withdraw.

8. Angela Duckworth, "Can Perseverance Be Taught?" *Big Questions Online,* August 5, 2013, https://www.bigquestionsonline.com /content/can-perseverance-be-taught.

9. Tough, *How Children Succeed,* 9–11.

10. Tough, *How Children Succeed,* 12.

11. Tough, *How Children Succeed,* 30.

12. Tough, *How Children Succeed,* 31–32.

13. Tough, *How Children Succeed,* 36.

14. Tough, *How Children Succeed,* 18.

15. Tough, *How Children Succeed,* 16.

16. Tough, *How Children Succeed,* 38.

17. Tough, *How Children Succeed,* 20.

18. Bryk, Lee, and Holland, *Catholic Schools and the Common Good,* 278.

19. Bryk, Lee, and Holland, *Catholic Schools and the Common Good,* 286–87.

20. Bryk, Lee, and Holland, *Catholic Schools and the Common Good,* 290–91.

21. Jacob Palma was tragically killed by a hit-and-run driver as he was crossing the street in a crosswalk following a youth group meeting at his church on the evening of Friday, September 13, 2013.

22. Tough, *How Children Succeed,* 90–91.

23. David Conley, "Metacognitive Learning Skills: Rethinking the Notion of 'Noncognitive,'" *Educational Policy Improvement Center,* accessed March 12, 2014, http://www.epiconline.org/Issues /metacognition/.

24. Tough, *How Children Succeed,* 64.